GORDON
STRACHAN'S
SOCCER
SKILLS

GORDON STRACHAN'S

SOCCER SKILLS

Specially commissioned
photography by
Action Plus

A COMPLETE

STEP-BY-STEP

GUIDE

CHANCELLOR
PRESS

Acknowledgements

There are many people to thank for their help and co-operation in putting together this book. In particular I would like to thank my old friend and playing colleague, Mark McGhee, for allowing us to use Reading FC's excellent training facilities at Pangbourne and, of course, the ground's owner Martin Deaner. Many thanks also to the boys of the Reading youth team (pictured below) who provided enthusiastic and skilful assistance throughout the photographic session. A particular thank you is due to Alfred Galustian of *Coerver Coaching* whose youth coaching methods I have long admired. Alfred provided invaluable assistance with regard to the dribbling exercises and methods of beating a man and any young player would be well advised to attend a Coerver coaching clinic or playing camp. Thanks too to Graham Morgan of *Adidas* who provided the players' kits and indeed my own! Lastly many thanks to Don Warters of the *Yorkshire Evening Post* who helped me to put my ideas into words during the course of several enjoyable afternoons.

First published in Great Britain in 1993
by Chancellor Press an imprint of
Reed Consumer Books Limited
Michelin House, 81 Fulham Road, London SW3 6RB
and Auckland, Melbourne, Singapore and Toronto

Copyright © 1993 Reed International Books Limited

ISBN 1 851 52537 8

A catalogue record for this book is available
from the British Library

Printed in Great Britain

CONTENTS

Introduction 6

Gordon Strachan Factfile 8

Kicking the Ball 10-11

Passing 12-19

The First Touch 20-25

Playing in Attack 26-27

Shooting at Goal 28-33

Dribbling and Close Control 34-37

Beating Your Opponent 38-43

Playing in Midfield 44-45

Advanced Shooting Skills 46-49

Crossing the Ball 50-51

Heading the Ball 52-53

Tackling and Winning the Ball 54-55

Closing Down Your Opponent 56-57

Taking a Throw-in 58-61

Taking Penalties 62-65

Taking Free Kicks 66-69

Taking Corners 70-73

Playing in Defence 74-75

Gordon's Best Team 76-77

Preparation and Attitude 78-79

Index 80

INTRODUCTION

I am very grateful to the publishers for giving me the opportunity to say in public what I have been thinking and talking about privately for years. Preparing this book has given me the chance to take a closer look at coaching and I have come to realise just how much I enjoy it. I have been a fully qualified coach for years but during the 'shoots' for the illustrations, I have to say that my enthusiasm got going again.

Soccer is a wonderful game and if I can add to it by coaching when I stop playing then I will be

more than delighted. I believe that if we can merge the qualities that we have in abundance in British football – honesty, bravery, a will to win – with a topping-up of the skill level, then our game could be a world beater once again.

One of my biggest worries about the game is producing young players for the top level. In a nutshell, I believe children in Britain play organised 11-a-side football too early. Basically, children under ten years old should not play the 11-a-side game. It would be far better for players this young to play 7-a-side football. This would allow them to play in all positions, on smaller pitches, with smaller goals. Youngsters playing 11-a-side tend to be selected in one position and will probably remain in that position for the rest of their career. In my view, that is far too early for a youngster to be moulded into a certain role. By allowing them to gain experience of different roles – which they will get in 7-a-side matches – youngsters will develop more all round skills which will benefit them in whatever position they eventually choose.

There is too much pressurised football played these days. When I was a kid I played for at least four hours a day without any strain. I found out by myself when it was time to pass the ball and when it was time to dribble it. When I was nine years old I did not need anyone to shout and scream at me. A call from a teammate or a kick on the shins from an opponent made me aware of when to get rid of the ball!

As a youngster I was allowed to think for myself but I find that, today, young children are not allowed to do that. Street football was a very popular pastime when I was young, but this is not so anymore and I would like to think that 7-a-side football could replace the street football we used to play. In my young days, naturally gifted players started in street football – not in a

league for Under 8s. No one taught me to play offside (thankfully at that age) or pressurise the ball – I found it all out for myself.

I am not against youngsters being coached at an early age – but that should be done on an individual level. Matches are for enjoyment and self-expression. We can show the young how to develop individually and I hope that this book will help in that direction.

When I watch youngsters training I feel they do too much running. I see people making young kids do sit-ups and press-ups, which is nonsense because kids of that early age should not even think of doing press-ups. Their muscular development is limited at that stage and doing press-ups could result in them suffering a hernia, muscle strains and other ailments later on in their careers.

Managers who look after young teams have told me that they do not have sufficient equipment. They say they have only three or four footballs and, in the same breath almost, ask me to go along to a prize giving to present 300 medals – where did the money come from for those I ask myself? Surely that money could be better used for equipment to help develop individual skills.

I suppose it is not surprising that coaches of young teams and their young players like to win medals. But I would say to such coaches that they would experience far more pleasure from seeing one of their players became a professional. You never know, the player might even go on to write a book saying that the guy who helped him most was his first coach!

Parents can be of help by not pushing their children too hard. I've seen parents who put an incredible amount of pressure on their children to become footballers. But no matter how much shouting they do from the touch line it will never make their kids better footballers. I sometimes see 10 year olds make rash tackles on other boys because their fathers had wound them up so much that they simply flew into tackles.

Another thing that annoys me are those coaches who shout at kids during a game, telling them in a frenzied manner what they should have done. The best way to tell them is after the game – in a calm and civilised manner.

Most of the moves or skills we have tried to show in this book are ones you can practise with your friends and teammates, and you do not need to be under the supervision of anyone.

Having got all that off my chest, it only remains for me to say that I hope you enjoy the book. It has been great fun compiling it and I hope you will find that it helps you to become a better player. If just one or two of you become professional footballers it will have been well worth the time and effort put in.

Gordon Strachan

GORDON STRACHAN
FACTFILE

Date of Birth	**February 9, 1956**
Birth Place	**Edinburgh**
Height	**5ft 6in**
Weight	**10st 8lbs**
Clubs	**Dundee 1972-77**
	Aberdeen 1977-84
	Manchester United 1984-89
	Leeds United 1989 to present day

Gordon Strachan's Goalscoring Record in League, Cup and European Football

	GOALS	PENALTIES
Scottish League		
Dundee	13	3
Aberdeen	54	29
Scottish FA Cup	7	3
Scottish League Cup	20	9
English League		
Manchester United	29	7
Leeds United	30	15
FA Cup	1	1
European Club Competitions	10	6
Total in club League and Cup competitions	164	73
International Goals	4	2
Career total	168	75

Captain Gordon Strachan with the Barclays League Championship Trophy won by Leeds United in 1991-92

INTERNATIONAL HONOURS

50 full caps for Scotland; place in Scotland's Soccer Hall of Fame; Scotland Under 21s and Under 23s, Scotland Youth, Scotland Schoolboys.

First full international game: v Northern Ireland in Belfast 1980.

Last full international v Finland at Hampden Park 1992.

Gordon scores Scotland's only goal in the 1986 World Cup finals in Mexico, against West Germany.

Brief Career Resume

Gordon is the only British player to have been voted Player of the Year in both England and Scotland. As an attacking, wide midfield player he won 50 Scottish international caps. He has won both Scottish and English FA Cup Winners' medals and also League Championship medals in both countries. As an Aberdeen player he won a European Cup Winners' Cup medal and after moving from Manchester United to Leeds in 1989 was a determining influence in hauling them from the bottom of the English Second Division to the First Division Championship within three seasons. Gordon is a fully qualified SFA coach and still, at the age of 37, a major influence in the Leeds United midfield.

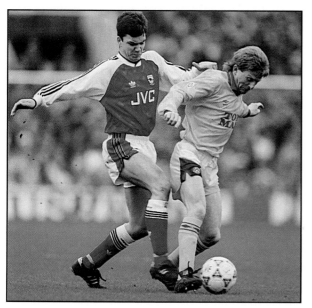

Gordon (Leeds) shields the ball from David Hillier (Arsenal) in a First Division match, 1991-92.

Gordon in his Manchester United days playing against Liverpool in the 1985 FA Cup competition.

KICKING THE BALL

It might be stating the obvious to say that the two most important assets a soccer player has are his feet. Other parts of the body such as the head, knees or chest are also used to propel or control the ball, but the major part of any soccer game involves kicking the ball with the feet.

Kicking a ball, you might think, is a straightforward action that comes naturally – and to most people it does. But if you are to have full control over the ball and make it go where you want it to go and at the right speed, there is more

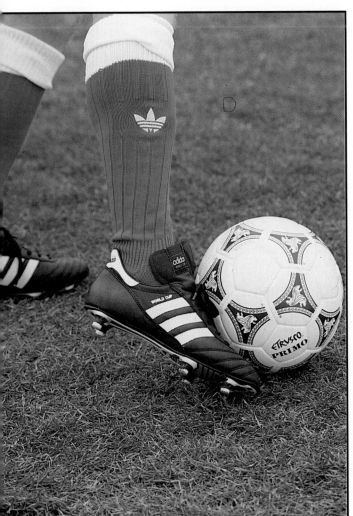

to kicking a football than merely bringing your foot into contact with it.

First of all, it really makes sense to look after your feet. Make sure that you wear boots that are comfortable. Boots that are too small will damage your feet, give you blisters and generally make life painful. Equally, you should not wear boots that are too big. Once you have found the style or manufacture of boots which is good for you, my tip is to stick with these boots all the time.

There are lots of different styles of boots on the market these days. Some look very flashy and very colourful, but don't be tempted merely by the way the boots look. It is how they feel when you have them on your feet that counts. I stuck with the same brand of boots all my career once I found the style that suited me best. Comfort is of paramount importance to me and my feet and it should be to you and your feet.

You should ensure that you keep your feet clean and you should make sure that your toenails are not allowed to grow too long or are not cut too short. Either way, they can cause you discomfort and problems.

Having made sure that your feet are in good condition, we come at last to the important part of actually kicking the ball. There are certain points to bear in mind when kicking a football. Generally speaking you should not kick the ball with your toes. Use the inside of the foot, the outside or the instep.

The most accurate way of kicking the ball is to use the inside of the foot. As I am right-

I am kicking the ball with the instep, the most used kicking zone. It is the part of the foot which combines power with accuracy and is used for quick free kicks, chips, crosses, long passes, etc.

footed, I use the left side of my right foot to propel the ball or direct it where I would like it to go. Left-footed players would use the right side of their left foot. Of course, if you are 'two-footed' then you have a big advantage.

When using the outside of the foot it is difficult to send the ball straight. You will usually find that the ball will 'curl' in flight so it is not quite as easy to direct the ball as it is using the inside of the foot. Curling the ball in some situations can be an advantage, however, and this is a skill dealt with later.

The way to get plenty of pace or power on the ball is by kicking it with the top of the foot or instep (the middle section of the foot which forms the arch between the ankle and toes). Goalkeepers use this technique to get the ball downfield and defenders to clear an attack. When strikers blast the ball into the net it is more often than not by using the top of the foot.

It is essential for the good of your game that you try to master the various methods there are of kicking a ball. Certain things are common to them all. Make sure that you keep your eye on the ball all the time. If you are having a shot at goal or passing to a team-mate you should have a good idea where the target is without the need for a last-second check, so watch the ball until you have completed your kick.

Finally, it is important to realise the part played by the non-kicking foot. It should be next to the ball when the ball is struck and not ahead of or behind it. This foot determines your balance and the power you can get into the shot.

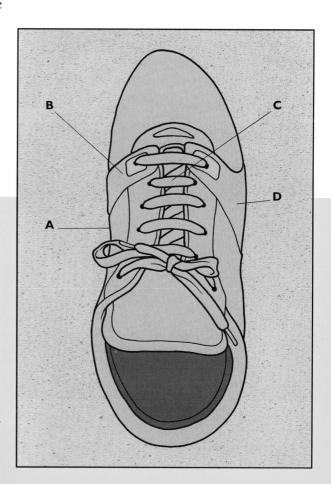

Kicking area of the foot

A The inside: Used for playing accurate low passes or placing the ball in a specific spot.

B The instep: The most used kicking zone. Chips, crosses, shots of any length can be made with instep.

C The top: The most powerful contact area. A ball driven with the top of the foot will travel with maximum force. This area is used when volleying at goal or clear of trouble.

D The outside: A bending volley, a curving chip or a ball controlling area – that is the role of the outside of the foot.

PASSING 1

Throughout my career I have always worked on the theory that, no matter how good you may think you are at a certain skill, there is always room for improvement.

I would hate anyone to think I am big-headed but I believe I am blessed with having a good 'touch' or 'feel' on the ball. Yet this belief has never stopped me in the 20 years I have played the game at professional level from trying to become a better passer of the ball. Passing is an absolutely basic skill that must be mastered – whatever position you play in.

The game is played at a much faster pace these days than it used to be. You are given much less space and very little time on the ball. When I began all those years ago there was a lot more room for errors but that is not the case now. One way that you can get more time to think about

your next move is if you receive an accurate pass that can be quickly controlled.

So you can see that passing needs to be spot on – and this applies to whatever level you might be playing at. When you find that you can pass the ball accurately it will not only give you a tremendous feeling of satisfaction and enjoyment, you will also have become a far more valuable team member. Your colleagues will soon learn to appreciate that a pass from you will arrive where they want it and can control it. A ball is much easier to control with the feet – after all we are talking about football not head tennis!

The great passers of the ball such as Chris Waddle, Glenn Hoddle, Graeme Souness, Ray Wilkins, and Kenny Dalglish were all invaluable members of their respective teams – and favourites with their fans.

1 The ball is at my feet and I am shielding it from the defender while I prepare to hit it with the inside of my foot.

2 Now I have made the pass. Note that the ball is on the ground. Passes along the ground are best because they are easier for the receiver to control than those arriving through the air.

Be upright and relaxed and try to make sure you do not lean backwards when making contact with the ball otherwise you will not be in full control of the pass. The pace of this pass is all important. If it is played too slow your opponent has a chance of intercepting; too fast and it makes control for the player receiving it more difficult.

THE SIDEFOOT PASS

Whenever you can, over the shorter distances, use the sidefoot pass. This is the easiest and most accurate method of passing the ball and it allows you to send the ball along the ground while shielding it from your opponent. But always remember your job isn't over when you've made the pass. You must keep the momentum of the movement going. Run into position for a return pass or run into space where you will be available to continue the attack, or where you will draw a marker from a colleague. Don't stand there admiring yourself but move off quickly and get back in the game!

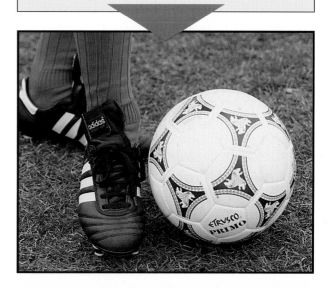

3 My teammate is now in possession and I have moved forward to create more space just in case my teammate wants to use me for a return pass.

Gordon's GEMS

● When passing, always try to keep yourself between the defender and the ball to give him as little chance as possible of taking the ball from you.

● When tying your bootlaces, make sure the knot is on the top of the foot. If it slips down the side it can affect the pass when you play the ball side footed.

● Don't relax after passing but move into space and keep in the game.

PASSING 2

CHIPPED PASS

I like to think of the chip as an attacking skill because it can be used to score a goal, beat a defensive 'wall' and put a teammate into an attacking position. It can open up the tightest-marking defences. But it can also be used if you are under pressure in a defensive situation.

Both the outside and the inside of the foot – as well as the top – can be used when you make a 'stab' at the ball but to play this difficult pass with a reasonable degree of accuracy you must practice long and hard. Even if you think you are blessed with skills, there is still a need to work at this aspect of your game.

The chip can be very rewarding, as one of its main uses is in scoring goals by lifting the ball over the goalkeeper's head if he happens to be out of position too far off his line.

TECHNIQUE

The way to play the chip shot is to make a 'stab' at the ball and get your foot underneath it, as you see me doing in the picture below. Contact is made with the lower part of the instep and this has the effect of putting backspin on the ball and making it float away. There should be only a short backlift of the kicking leg and hardly any follow through when making this pass.

Gordon's GEMS

● Where possible, I prefer to use the more easily controlled ground pass to the more ambitious chip pass, reserving the chip for occasions when the less risky ground pass is blocked.

● When you make up your mind that you are going to chip, make the pass confidently and you will have a better chance of playing it well.

● Don't give your opponent a chance of intercepting the pass. Make sure you chip the ball high enough over his head.

1 As I prepare to kick the ball, my head is nearly over it. But I take care not to get my head too far forward otherwise I will not be able to get the ball up high enough.

2 My kicking foot has come through and lifted the ball into the air but my eyes are still fixed on the ball. Taking your eye off the ball is fatal for any passing move.

3 I lean back slightly to see the ball pass high over the defender on its way to my teammate. Only now have I permitted myself to watch the result of the pass.

4 The ball is landing at the feet of my teammate, while the opponent is helpless. It is satisfying to see the ball obey my wishes. A job well done!

BENDING THE BALL

One of the points which I will keep stressing in this book is the need to practise. I make no apologies for repeating this. In my view there is no such thing as the perfect footballer but practice is a valuable aid in helping you to achieve your potential no matter at what level you may be playing the game.

If you are right-footed, as I am, and you use the outside of your foot to 'graze' the left half of the ball it should curve away to the right (if you are left-footed and use this particular method the ball will curve to the left). Should you decide to use the inside of your foot to 'graze' the right half of the ball it will curve away to the left. (The opposite will apply if you are left-footed.)

When you make this shot or pass make sure that the non-kicking foot is in line with the ball and that you follow through with the kicking foot in just the same way as a golfer does when he makes a tee-shot.

TECHNIQUE

Keep your eyes on the ball and with the outside of your kicking foot make contact with the side of the ball. It is vital in making this pass that you follow through with the kicking leg. If you have done this correctly then the ball should spin as it goes through the air and this in turn makes the ball 'curve' on its way to the player who is due to receive the ball. Once you have mastered this technique you can use it to very good effect during games – it is one of the most effective ways of causing your opponents problems.

Gordon's GEMS

● Make sure you exaggerate the follow through with your kicking leg when making this pass.

● This is not an easy pass to make so practise it as often as you can.

● Do not under-hit this pass. One of the most frustrating things in the game for players and spectators is to see the ball given away because the strength of the pass is wrong.

1 A defender is ready to challenge, so I decide to 'bend' the ball round him to my teammate on the wing. As you can see I have followed through with the foot after striking the ball.

2 The ball 'curves' round the challenging player and towards the winger who has moved forward to meet it as soon as he saw my intention.

3 The winger is now ahead of the defender and has managed to receive my pass without being tackled and he is ready to take the ball down the wing or pass inside.

PASSING 4

THE WALL PASS

There are various ways in which you can attempt to beat an opponent – one of the most effective being the 'wall' pass. This gets you past him without the need to dribble, and is much easier and less risky than dribbling.

In effect, you use a colleague as if he were a wall, passing the ball to him and collecting the 'rebound'. As with most things in football, timing is of the greatest importance. I first gained knowledge of this particular move by watching a couple of guys when I first started out in the game at Dundee. Jocky Scott and Gordon Wallace were very good at it and I soon realised how effective this move can be.

It is easy to use, provided you time it right. If you are too far away from the defender when you attempt the wall pass, then the defender has the time to turn and win possession. Alternatively, if you are too close, the defender can stick out a leg to intercept or deflect the pass.

Of course, you need to have a teammate in a good position to knock the ball to so that you can run on to take a return pass.

Opponents do not stand about like dummies while you execute your pretty moves around them, so it is necessary to catch the defender flat-footed. You do this with a swift change of pace. While the defender is reacting, turning and taking up the chase, your sudden sprint forward should leave him for dead.

When I was a youngster I was known as a dribbler, but when I joined Dundee I soon learned the value of passing. I had joined them from school eager to learn and make a career playing soccer and I soon found what a help it was to study older and more experienced players. You should listen to any advice such players may

1 I make a determined run at the defender and just as I get near to him I pass the ball to my teammate who is in a forward position.

2 Once the pass has been made and the ball is on the way to my teammate I accelerate and make a run forward myself.

have to offer. You can decide afterwards whether their advice feels right for you personally but you have nothing to lose by listening and a great deal to gain.

When I was at Dundee I nursed an ambition that one day during a match I would make two successive wall passes on my way to scoring a goal. Years later, when playing for Aberdeen against Kilmarnock, I managed it. In a run from the half way line I played three wall passes and finished off by shooting, with my left foot. To this day I think that was the best goal I have ever scored. I had probably run half the length of the field, had four touches of the ball and scored – which just goes to show the value of the wall pass. It saves a lot of running with the ball and can pay a rich dividend. But the angle of the pass, the speed of the ball and the touch from the target man – the 'wall' – has to be right, as has the timing of your run.

Gordon's GEMS

● It is essential that your pass is accurate if you are to make the most of what is a very productive move.

● Increasing your pace is a must if your marker is to be caught flat-footed.

● Make sure the ball is played wide enough to prevent the defender sticking out a leg to block the ball.

● Be alert to the possibility of acting as a 'wall' yourself for one of your teammates carrying the ball forward.

3 My teammate has taken up possession and immediately knocks the ball into space behind my marker for me to run on to.

4 The marker has been caught flat-footed. Having moved forward, I am ready to take up possession again and carry on towards goal.

You often hear commentators on the television say that a particular player seems to have a lot of time or always seems to find himself space or is never rushed. This all comes down to the fact that the player's first touch on the ball is a good one and he is able to control the ball quickly even on receiving a poor pass. Manchester United and former Aberdeen manager Alex Ferguson always used to say about me that my first touch on the ball was good.

As I have said before, time and space are rare commodities in the modern game when defenders are so fit and fast. A good first touch can allow you that time and space. It might only be a second or two but that is all you need to be able to get a good pass away, turn a defender or take a snap shot.

As far as I am concerned, initial control is one of the easier skills to learn. Once you feel comfortable about receiving the ball from any angle, you can develop this skill to a higher level. Then, instead of the ball bouncing away from you when you receive it from a teammate, you can take it and, in one movement, swivel round to face the way you want to go rather than have to use maybe as many as three touches to make the turn.

I learnt to do this as a schoolboy by kicking the ball for hours and hours against two brick walls and even when I became a professional I used this very basic method to continue to improve my skills.

All you need are two walls at right angles and a ball – and, of course, the determination and patience to be prepared to put in plenty of practice. The method is simple and effective.

What you do is kick the ball against one wall and when it comes back turn and hit it against the other wall. Do this with your feet, head or other parts of the body. Keep on doing that non-stop for about 20 minutes and you will probably get over 1,000 touches on the ball. This is the beauty of the method because it is impossible to get that number of touches on the ball by playing 90 minutes in a football match.

TRAPPING THE BALL

The trap is a fundamental method of controlling a bouncing ball. I get my foot high to bring it down on the ball.

CONTROLLING THE BALL WITH THE INSIDE OF THE LEG

1 The ball is bouncing towards me and I let it hit the inside of my raised leg. I ride the ball back slightly along the line of flight to bring it under control.

2 After hitting my leg the ball drops to the ground and I am in control of it, ready to do whatever I want with it.

If you can get right your initial control of the ball – the first touch – then you will have gone a long way to being an effective footballer.

On the other hand, if you do not master this particular skill you could struggle in today's game because there are some teams around who have players whose primary purpose is to try to stop you playing, or 'close you down' as they say nowadays.

If you cannot trap a ball properly or control it quickly, these players will blot you out of the game by marking up tight and stepping in to take the ball whenever you let it slip out of your control.

CONTROLLING ON THE CHEST

One of the most important points to bear in mind when attempting to control the ball with the chest is to be relaxed. I would far rather try to control the ball with the chest than head it. That might have something to do with the fact that I have never been able to head the ball all that well! But the chest is, after all, a large and safe area on which to control the football.

As with heading, you must keep your eyes firmly fixed on the ball. As it comes towards you through the air try to pick up the flight, and anticipate where it will drop.

Watching closely, move into a good position and be up on your toes and leaning back slightly as the ball makes contact with your chest. Try to 'cushion' the impact or allow it to hit you naturally.

When the ball hits your chest it will then begin to drop and the quicker you gain control with your feet the better. It is important that you complete this movement smoothly and quickly.

If you are a defender it is possible for you to deflect the ball away from an attacker by turning the chest as the ball hits it – as Steve Bruce does so well for Manchester United.

1 I am up on my toes and leaning back slightly as the ball drops onto my chest.

2 The ball is on a downward path and I am about to let it hit my raised leg.

3 Now the ball is down at my feet and that's where I like it. Control is better there.

1 The ball is on its way to me and I make sure I watch it closely.

2 The leg I am using to control the ball with is angled down and that's the direction in which I am looking too.

3 The ball is on the ground and I am already passing it on.

CONTROLLING ON THE THIGH

The technique for taking control of the ball on the thigh is much the same as that for controlling it on the chest.

You will make a mess of it, however, unless you follow the flight of the ball closely. As the ball arrives, you need to be in position with your thigh at an angle of about 45 degrees to the ground. Watch the ball right onto your thigh. When it hits your thigh it will bounce down and you then need to be ready to keep the game flowing either by immediately moving off with the ball at your feet or by playing it on to a teammate.

Speed of thought and action are vital ingredients in soccer and if you can complete this particular move smoothly and swiftly so much the better.

Gordon's GEMS

● Keeping your eyes on the ball is vital when controlling the ball with your chest or thigh.

● It is important to be relaxed. The ball is hard but it will not hurt when it hits the chest or thigh.

● Execute these moves swiftly and you will often avoid being tackled or bumped around.

● When bringing the ball down make sure your raised leg is angled down otherwise the ball will bounce back up from your knee and you will lose tight control.

CONTROLLING WITH THE HEAD AND PASSING ON

I have to be honest and confess that heading the ball is not one of the stronger points in my game. I have managed to score quite a lot of goals in my career but I think that in 21 years of playing I managed to score only four with my head.

However, I certainly admire those players who can head the ball well, such as Welsh international and Leeds United midfield player Gary Speed. He is not a really tall lad but his timing is excellent, and that is the secret of being a good header of the ball.

Heading is not only a matter of scoring goals or clearing from defence – sometimes a pass will come to you head-high, and you will have to bring it under control, move off with it yourself or direct a controlled headed pass to a teammate.

Once you have decided to use your head to control the ball, you must keep your eye on the ball, be positive and not allow yourself to be deflected from what you intend to do by the closeness of opponents.

The front part of your forehead is where contact with the ball should be made. Obviously you must keep your eyes open to ensure you connect properly. The skull is tough and a properly headed ball does not hurt.

Before making contact you must know just what you are going to do and in which direction you want to move once the ball has arrived. As the ball hits your head try to 'cushion' the blow and at the point of impact turn slightly in the direction you wish to move off in, or in the direction you wish to head the ball.

Do not jump unnecessarily. Some players jump when just as good a contact could be made if they stayed on their feet, when they would be able to move off quickly into a new position.

These days, with space on the ground at a premium – crowded midfields and penalty areas – some teams use 'target men' to whom the ball is passed in the air and whose job it is to flick it on or knock it down for a teammate. Many goals are scored this way, so it can be seen that control with the head is a vital part of the game.

There has been no finer recent example of the value of the headed pass than at Manchester United where those excellent central defenders, Gary Pallister and Steve Bruce, played a key role in helping Alex Ferguson's side take the Championship in the Premier League's inaugural 1992-93 season. Their defensive headers were always directed forwards towards colleagues with the aim of putting United on the attack.

Gordon's GEMS

● Concentration is again the name of the game – keep your eye on the ball.

● Make up your mind about what you are going to do with the ball and be positive.

● Balance is important, so make sure you are relaxed and not leaning too far forward.

1 As the ball comes to me I position myself so that I jump to allow the ball to make contact with my forehead.

2 When I head the ball I turn my head slightly at the same time to enable me to direct the ball in the direction of my teammate.

3 My teammate is about to take possession and I begin to move forward so that I am ready should he wish to pass back to me.

PLAYING IN ATTACK

Because most goals are scored by players who operate in attack, this section of the team is usually seen as the most glamorous.

Certainly, supporters love players who score goals and as far as I am concerned there is no finer feeling in the game than scoring a goal.

Strikers come in all shapes and sizes, and employ different methods, but what is common to them all of course, is a hunger and an eye for goal. Pace, height and strength are also useful assets, as well as a willingness to take the sort of

Mick Harford – a perfect example of the tall, strong 'target man' who spreads panic amongst defenders.

knocks that occur when everybody is at full stretch in the penalty area. England strikers Ian Wright and Alan Shearer are prime examples of the modern day goalscorer. Both are strong and extremely athletic, with plenty of pace and confidence.

A different type of striker is what we call the 'target man', a less mobile player than Wright. One of the best of recent times is Mick Harford. I think he realised early on in his career that he was best suited to being a target man – a player who makes space for himself for teammates to cross the ball to. He is a midfield player's dream because he makes himself so readily available and his strength and sheer determination make him a major problem for defenders.

The target man takes a lot of knocks from burly defenders as he waits for balls to be played in from the flanks or midfield. So if you fancy this role, obviously you will need to be big and strong to compete with them.

In addition to scoring goals yourself, if you are a target man you should also look to make scoring chances for teammates by knocking balls down to those who run into the penalty area or six-yard box.

Strikers such as Ian Rush and Gary Lineker were players who caused havoc in front of their opponents' goal. They were the kings of the six yard box because they were so alert to scoring opportunities and quick in their ability to get the ball into the net. If this is your role you cannot relax. You must always be concentrating, always trying to anticipate the unexpected and always on your toes ready to pounce. Your main asset is your ability to poach two yards on slower-witted defenders.

Wingers have virtually disappeared from the game these days. Those attackers who play on the flanks are known as wide men or, as Ron

Atkinson always referred to me, wide receivers.

Whereas the wingers of yesterday would wait for the ball to be played to them, today the men who play 'wide' are expected to attack, defend and often go in search of the ball. Trevor Steven and Chris Waddle are current players who do their best work up and down the flanks. So, if you look upon yourself as a present day wide player, you must follow their example and be prepared to put in a lot of running.

Remember that, although the strike force is

Perhaps the greatest modern day centre forward, Holland's Marco Van Basten, is big but skilful . . . and a clinical finisher.

A more complete player than the pure 'target man', Blackburn's Alan Shearer is quick and skilful.

where individual skills possibly must have expression, even here football is still a team game. The wide man might beat his man continuously and make dazzling runs down the wing, but his work will come to nothing if nobody is available in the middle to convert it into goals. It is no good the target man losing his marker, or a mobile striker bursting into space in the penalty area or making a diagonal run, if nobody passes the ball to him.

Be aware of the needs of the team. If the full-back sprints down the wing the wide man should cover for him. If a midfielder makes a break down the centre, the central strikers should support him by drawing markers or making themselves available.

The strikers get most applause – it is only fair they share the work!

SHOOTING AT GOAL 1

SHOOTING AT GOAL FROM CLOSE RANGE

When you are shooting from close range, it is essential that you get your effort on target. There is nothing worse than seeing somebody thrash at the ball six yards out only for it to go past the wrong side of the post or over the bar.

Admittedly it is great to see the ball crashing into the back of the net. All youngsters love to see that happen, especially when playing at school with proper nets for the first time.

But it is not always necessary to blast the ball in, as all the top strikers will readily tell you. You will find as much enjoyment and satisfaction from side-footing the ball or merely tapping it into the goal when that is really all that is needed to score a goal. And of course a controlled tap cuts down the chance of accidents. If, as the ball comes across the goal, you are unlucky enough to get a bad bounce or a bobble at the last minute, you then have that split second to adjust because, by shaping up for a tap in, you have more control over your movement than if you were just going to thrash the ball.

Of course, many close-in goals (like the majority of mine!) are scored by instinct and reflex action. There is hardly time to think as a foot is prodded out to score. But if you think of

1 Photographed from the back of the net, I have knocked the ball forward and, chasing after it, I have managed to get away from the defender.

2 My run is timed so that I meet the ball with the inside of my favoured right foot to enable me to score with a sidefoot shot.

the many goals scored by such players as Gary Lineker, the common factor is that they were always in the right position. Anticipation is what leads to many close-range goals. Always be alert to what is going on and what might happen. Always have rebounds in mind. Try to guess where the ball might go and get there too!

Always be ready to try a shot when close to goal and do not mind if you miss. Even the best strikers miss a lot. One goal makes up for a dozen near misses.

Strikers should get into a mood where it is natural to do things early. Dithering is the greatest crime when a close-in chance arises. So cultivate a frame of mind where you don't need to think – as soon as the ball arrives, you act.

I still find it as great a thrill scoring a goal these days as I did when I first came into the game as a teenager with Dundee all those years ago. The fun of scoring always makes all the hard work and knocks that preceded it seem worthwhile.

When I find myself in a situation for a close range shot – and by close range I mean somewhere about eight yards from goal – I try to remain cool, calm and collected and go for placement and a controlled strike. There is nothing to be gained from panicking – going for a really hard strike can cut down on accuracy and control.

From my own experience of scoring goals from close range I have also found that the best chance of beating the keeper is by hitting the ball along the ground.

3 The ball is on its way into the net. The job is done and I am turning away to celebrate!

Gordon's
GEMS

● When trying to beat the goalkeeper, aim low. A shot at his waist level is easier for him to save than one on the ground.

● Don't panic in front of goal. Remain calm and make sure you get your shot on target.

● Never blast the ball when there is no need to. You have more control over the ball if you are not trying to blast it.

SHOOTING AT GOAL 2

LONG-RANGE SHOOTING

Because there is so much good defensive play nowadays, especially by teams who push out quickly to play offside, it is necessary to score a good percentage of goals by long-range shooting.

Not being known for my long distance shooting, I must refer to others for examples of this valuable skill. Probably the best in our game just now is Leeds United's Scottish international midfield player Gary McAllister. A goal he scored against Arsenal in an FA Cup tie at Elland Road in the 1992-93 season was a fine example of a great long range shot.

Long-range shooting really needs only the application of basic kicking skills. If you can kick powerfully, then you can shoot from long range. The added requirement, perhaps, is an awareness of the situation and quick thinking. Defenders are always trying to close strikers down to prevent them getting in a shot – the striker's job therefore is to outwit them and take the defence (including the goalkeeper) by surprise.

A long-range shot, unless it's a chip, should be powerful. For maximum power, the non-kicking leg should be alongside the ball at the moment of impact, the head directly over the ball. The top of the foot imparts most power, but of course you cannot always choose the optimum position for shooting – you might be forced to volley or half-volley, or strike the ball with the instep or outside of the foot, or be forced to shoot with an opponent bearing down on you.

The main requirement is that, once you have decided to shoot, do it with conviction and confidence. Keep your eye on the ball and follow through after hitting it.

Just because you are further away from the goal, do not think that there is less chance of a surprise shot than when you are close in. In some ways, surprise is more important. A top-class goalkeeper will not be beaten easily from way out – surprising him gives you a better chance.

Obviously, you must try hard to get your shots on target, although I accept that there is a greater margin for error compared to shots from close range. Errors and mishaps can work in your favour, however. The shot may be deflected or the goalkeeper may be unsighted.

Basically, when shooting from a long distance you must aim for one of the corners of the goal. The best keepers are rarely beaten by a long shot which is close to them. You have to accept that not every long-range shot you attempt will be on target but my message to all budding long-range artists is: 'Don't be afraid to miss.'

Gordon's GEMS

● When trying a long-range shot don't be afraid of missing. Nothing ventured, nothing gained!

● Try to aim for one of the corners of the goal – it makes it more difficult for the keeper to get to the ball.

● Make up your mind and go for it. Never change your mind as you prepare to shoot.

1 Defenders are closing in fast and I haven't the pace to get away so I choose to try my luck with a shot at goal.

2 The goalkeeper is more to one side of the goal so I've aimed for the other side.

3 The defenders are on me but they're too late. The 'keeper has made a valiant attempt but it's another goal for me!

SHOOTING AT GOAL 3

One of the most satisfying goals of my career, scored for Scotland against Romania in 1986. Their keeper had strayed off his line and I left him stranded with a lob from the edge of the box.

CHIPPING THE KEEPER

A particularly satisfying way to score is with the chip shot or lob, using the same technique described earlier for the chipped pass.

You have to be positive in a situation like this, so once you have made up your mind you are going to attempt the chip, don't change it. Stick to that course of action.

When the keeper comes off his line and advances towards you, the opportunity is there for you to 'lift' or chip the ball high enough over his head so that he cannot reach it, but with only sufficient pace on the ball to allow it to drop behind him and into the net.

1 The ball is at my feet and I notice that the goalkeeper has advanced off his line.

2 I have chipped the ball high in the air, over the defenders, and it's on its way to goal.

JUST THE KEEPER TO BEAT

When you suddenly find yourself in a one-on-one situation with the goalkeeper you are faced with making a quick decision.

If you choose to try a shot on the run remember to hit the ball low and hard. It is often a help to glance at the goalkeeper when you are about ten yards from him and you will usually find he has come out to narrow the angle.

Should that be the case, a split second or so before you shoot, touch the ball slightly to one side. This tends to put the keeper off and you will have a better chance of beating him.

As an example of this I remember playing for Manchester United against Liverpool about six years ago in a game which ended level at 3-3. As I ran through the Liverpool defence I had only Bruce Grobbelaar to beat. It was probably the longest run at goal I had had in my life and Alan Hansen, one of the best defenders in the world, was closing in on me.

Grobbelaar, who can be a bit of an eccentric goalkeeper at times, stood there glaring at me but I kept cool and made up my mind what I was going to do. I chose the option of hitting the ball close to his feet. I think that if I had put it more to his side he might have got to the ball.

Anyway I succeeded and scored what was our equaliser and believe me it was a very satisfying moment for me!

Another way of beating the keeper is to make out you are going to fire into one corner by looking that particular way and, as the keeper then (you hope!) will anticipate you, you suddenly change direction and hit it into the other corner.

3 The goalkeeper sees the ball, realises he is off his line and begins to move back.

4 He has made a desperate effort to retrace his steps but it is too late. The ball has cleared him and dipped in under the bar.

DRIBBLING AND CLOSE CONTROL 1

Many people would say dribbling is a dying art but really it should not be as it's a skill that fans love to see and defenders don't!

In this age of tight marking and solid defences, there is nothing better than watching a player who can dribble his way past opponents. It is also extremely effective.

DEVELOPING THE CUT AWAY

There will be many times during a game when you find yourself face to face with a defender or an opponent – in a one-on-one situation, as we call it.

When faced with this problem, you have to make up your mind quickly whether you are going to pass to a teammate who may be in a better position and not so closely marked – or decide to take on the defender and beat him.

If you decide on (or are forced into) the second option the 'cut away' move is one way in which you can beat your opponent.

You have the ball at your feet and you are making progress. Everything is going well and then suddenly you discover a defender blocking your path and moving in to challenge you.

A key to beating this opponent with the 'cut away' is confidence and good control. As you get to him, throw your right foot past the ball (if you are right-footed that is) and with the outside of the foot drag the ball back. You will find that

your momentum will carry you past the ball a little. Turn your body to the right to shield the ball from him and move away.

In effect you have gone up to the defender and 'cut away' from him – hence the name we give to this particular movement.

The 'cut away' is similar in some respects to the 'cut' which I will explain in detail later in the book. For the 'cut' you approach the defender and then using the inside of your right foot 'cut' the ball inside as opposed to the outside of the right foot for the 'cut away'.

The best way of practising this move is with a friend, as the pictures on the opposite page show.

Gordon's **GEMS**

● You must keep close to the ball when attempting the 'cut away' move.

● Practise this move five minutes a day with your friend – you'll be amazed how it improves your game.

● Try practising this move using your weaker foot too, e.g. turn to the left instead of the right (as the centre player is doing in the pictures).

1 The attacker has a ball at his feet and sets off running towards the defender at three-quarter pace.

2 When the attacker is near the defender he throws his right foot past the ball in order to drag it back in the direction from which he came.

3 The attacker's momentum has carried him past the ball but at the same time he turns his body to present his back to the defender.

4 The attacker nearest the camera is perfectly positioned. His body is completely shielding the ball from the defender and he has it under control as he moves away.

DRIBBLING AND CLOSE CONTROL 2

DUMMYING OVER THE BALL

Dummying over the ball is probably as well known, if not better known, as 'the Rivelino move', named after the famous midfield player of the Brazilian World Cup-winning side in Mexico back in 1970. Everyone knew he would use this move at some time or other but he executed it so well that opponents found it virtually impossible to keep their balance when he did so.

As in the 'cut', or the 'Cruyff turn' which I describe later, it does not necessarily have to beat the opponent. The intention is to confuse him and buy a little time while keeping you and your team in possession. Nowhere is this better illustrated than in videos of the great Brazilian teams of the 1970s.

As big Ron Atkinson (manager of Aston Villa) would say, the dummying over the ball skill is not one that I have in my locker. Believe me, I wish I had but unfortunately it is something I never practised when I was younger.

Young readers should note that practising the various skills is better done now. For an old player like myself, practising something new can be uncomfortable. It certainly does not come as easily as it might have done years earlier, so take my tip and master the skills as best you can when you are young.

When you dummy over the ball you are trying to trick the defender into wrongly thinking you are going to kick the ball forward.

You throw your kicking foot over the ball,

unbalancing the defender. Make sure the outside of the foot is alongside the ball and drag the ball back. You are then able to move off in a different direction with the defender hopefully having been wrong footed and struggling to recover. At its, best this manoeuvre buys you a second or two of time to set up an attack.

On the page opposite is my favourite exercise for developing 'the Rivelino'. Four lads are shown practising the move with me as a defender in the middle.

Gordon's GEMS

● After eight attempts at this movement, change the man in the middle and carry on.

● When throwing the kicking foot past the ball really exaggerate the move. Make the defender react.

● Take it easy when practising. It is not necessary to dash about. Polish is more important than pace.

1 Four players, each with a ball, jog towards the defender in the middle.

2 As they arrive at the defender they throw their right foot past the ball, placing it at the side of the ball.

3 With the outside of the foot the attackers now take the ball at right angles away from the defender.

4 They now take the ball towards the next cone ready to face the defender and practise the move all over again.

BEATING YOUR OPPONENT 1

THE MATTHEWS

Every player, including defenders, should be able to dribble with the ball because this is a skill which can always be put to good use. But it is a skill which does not come easily to the majority of players, so once again practice is a must.

All you need is a ball and a bit of space. Run with the ball at your feet, sometimes quickly and sometimes a little slower. When you feel comfortable with the ball at your feet, set up a line of obstacles, ideally cones but anything will do, and weave your way between them as if they were opponents, keeping the ball as close to your toe as possible. Use both feet, and both instep and outside of the foot, until you are confident you can control the ball in tight situations. Keep at it and eventually you will get the 'feel' of the ball and become a better player.

Once you are able to control the ball in this way you are ready to add another skill to your repertoire – the feint, or as this move is probably more affectionately known in the game, 'the Matthews'.

This is one of the game's great moves and was made famous by one of the best players of all time, Stanley Matthews, who was knighted for his services to the game.

Matthews spent many years – his best – with

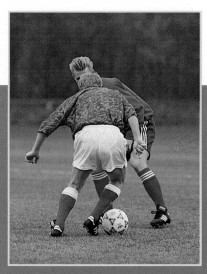

1 The defender has done his job and slowed me down by his challenge. I decide to use 'the Matthews'.

2 Making sure the ball is not too far from my foot, I 'feint' as if about to play the ball with my right instep, and move to the left.

3 Here the defender begins to lose his balance as he goes too far to his right and I begin to move away with the ball, using the outside of my right foot.

Blackpool when they were a top league side and is well remembered for the part he played in Blackpool's FA Cup final victory over Bolton Wanderers in 1953. His side were trailing 3-1 but hit back to win 4-3, Matthews showing the value of his close control and dribbling skills to make two of the last three goals.

Defenders in those days knew all about Matthews and his skills and what he was likely to do in a game, but they still found it impossible to handle him at times and that is the mark of a truly great player.

Basically, 'the Matthews' or 'the feint' is used for changing direction. It is a close control move for making defenders lose balance and is the most used move in the game by players who are in possession of the ball.

The more you use this when you are younger the more attuned to the movement your body will become. It is harder when you are older and your body is not as supple.

To make the most of 'the feint' you need to over emphasise your first movement. A good first move will tend to unbalance the defender and though you may not get by him with one move, if it buys you time and space on the ball by preventing him from tackling you or closing you down, then all well and good. This skill is a 'must' for players who want to go to the top, especially those who play in attack.

In addition to Matthews, George Best was one of the great exponents of this move and, for me, the present day favourite is Chris Waddle, shown executing the feint in the photograph above. Watch him closely and you will see that he really exaggerates the movement. You know what he is going to do. You swear you won't buy it during the game but, of course, you fall for it just like you have done in the past and you are left sprawling in the grass.

4 From a crouching position I decide to lift the ball over the foot of the defender's outstretched left leg with the outside of my right foot.

5 The defender has blown his chance and I dart away still in possession of the ball. He has to turn and cannot prevent me gaining several yards on him.

BEATING YOUR
OPPONENT 2

THE CUT

This is probably my favourite move in football – especially when I am going down the left side of the field. I have been making good use of this move for a long, long time – as long as I can remember in fact.

My liking for this particular move probably has something to do with the fact that it is one of the easiest to perform!

I remember years ago I was playing against Manchester City and at that time Neil McNab, one of my best friends, was in their side and I know he had wanted the City lads not to fall for the Gordon Strachan 'cut'.

He knew I loved the move and would at, some stage of the game, bring it into use and he had attempted to prepare all the City players for it. But very early in the game I got away on the left flank and as I ran towards the defender I made it look as though I was going to play the ball in-field and at the last moment I 'cut' the ball back and went away down the flank.

The defender had bought it and only five minutes of the game had gone. I could hear Neil screaming at his defender but the fact is that although this move is relatively simple and easy to do it is not one that is easy to defend against.

For some reason shorter players like myself are particularly good at this move, perhaps because they are closer to the ball and can turn quicker than more cumbersome defenders. That master of all skills George Best springs to mind, and Kenny Dalglish was another who could beat an opponent on a sixpence – and there has been a long line of small Scottish wingers from Jimmy Johnstone to Pat Nevin with this particular skill

When you play the 'cut' you have to be confident and feel comfortable on the ball and don't be worried about failing. On occasions the defender will stop you but it is worth remembering that the defender has a difficult job if you execute the move correctly.

And, of course, once the defender has committed himself and you are past him, he has no chance to recover. You have effectively cut your marker out of the game and bought precious seconds to set up an attack.

Gordon's GEMS

● Shout at a teammate in the middle of the field as though you are thinking of passing to him.

● Always exaggerate the first movement with the kicking leg.

● Increase your pace once the defender has fallen for the trick.

1 Looking down at the ball I try to make it look as though I am going to kick the ball into the middle of the field.

2 The defender stretches in an attempt to stop the pass but as my foot comes down I change direction and 'cut' the ball to the left, using the inside of my foot.

3 The defender is now completely off balance. He's beaten and I have pushed the ball away at right angles.

BEATING YOUR OPPONENT 3

THE 'CRUYFF' TURN

When I was beginning my career as a professional footballer, Johan Cruyff was taking over from Pele as the game's most exciting player. I think of him at his peak somewhere around the 1974 World Cup finals. It was the tournament where Scotland were eliminated without losing a match! Cruyff was unlucky, too, because Holland, whom he captained, were undoubtedly the team with the most flair and everybody's favourites, but they didn't quite click in the final and lost to West Germany.

Every player in that Dutch side from the fullbacks to the forwards had excellent skills on the ball and it was said that all of them could play in virtually any position on the field. The experts called the game they played 'total football'. But, even in this side, Cruyff's dribbling skills stood out. I particularly remember one move with which, three or four times during that tournament, he completely bamboozled his marker. To the spectator it looked like almost a conjuring trick. The move became known as the 'Cruyff turn', and many

1 I have lifted my right leg as if to strike the ball, and the opponent has moved to block the kick.

2 I am cutting the ball behind my standing foot with my right instep.

players have tried to incorporate it into their game. None manages it with quite the same breathtaking skill as Cruyff, but nevertheless many have succeeded in making it work. One player who had the confidence to use it was the current Sheffield Wednesday player/manager Trevor Francis, who was expert at the technique.

The move is used basically to change direction, sending the marker one way while you take the ball the other way. It can be used to take the ball across goal to create space for a shot, or it can be used down the wings where the marker is preventing you cutting in or is denying you space for a pass or cross.

Your opponent is beaten by selling him a dummy and by playing the ball behind your standing leg – not exactly a backheel but the nearest you will come to dribbling round your man with a backheel!

It is a spectacular skill but, like everything else, there is a time and place for it. If you have the will to practise it and perfect it, don't get carried away with it. Keep the element of surprise, and use it in a match only where it will make you most dangerous, or when there is no simpler alternative.

As with all skills, execute the move with confidence. Don't be afraid you will trip over your legs and look a fool. Your hours on the practice ground will ensure your success.

3 I quickly turn inside my opponent who is now completely wrong-footed and going in the wrong direction.

4 I accelerate away to the left leaving the opponent going the wrong way.

PLAYING IN MIDFIELD

Playing in midfield is a very demanding area of the game – I know that from 20 years experience of playing there!

Basically, you can put midfield players into two categories – the first being what I would term a creative one, a category where I would like to think I belong. Secondly there are those players who go in determined to win the ball, in which category I definitely do not include myself! Nowadays these players are known as 'ball-winners'.

When I was playing my football with Manchester United in the 1980s I was fortunate enough to play with two great midfield players in Bryan Robson and Norman Whiteside, who were always very busy and brave players and who combined something of both roles. They set a high standard for others to follow.

In my view, the most complete creative midfield player Britain has had over the last 15 years is Glenn Hoddle. Budding young midfield players who are keen to enhance their game would do well if they could get hold of a tape of him in action.

He could play equally well with either foot and was a joy to watch. He could hit short passes and long passes with almost equal accuracy. He could score great goals and generally he looked a very elegant player all the time. I have always been a bit envious of him because of that!

If you wish to become one of the great ball-winners – players who go in not merely to stop an opponent with a tackle but to come out of that tackle with the ball – then you need look no further than my Leeds United teammate David Batty.

David is brave and fearless in the tackle and is also skilful enough that when he comes away with the ball he has the ability to set another attack going.

If I say that the main role of a midfield player is as a support player, I am not talking down the role. In fact, you could say the opposite, because the complete midfielder has to be good at many things. He must support the defence – falling back, covering, making himself available for a pass from the back – and he must support the attack – providing support for the man with the

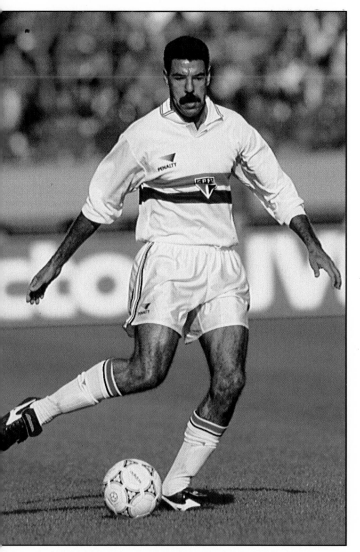

One of the best midfielders I ever played against – Toninho Cerezo of Brazil.

Glenn Hoddle always seemed unhurried on the ball and was a very accurate passer with either foot. He could also rifle in some superb long-range shots.

sorts of star midfielders around you for you to pick a favourite and base your game upon. My advice is to discover your own strengths and develop them, but also to work on your weaknesses. Your manager and colleagues will look up to you if you can do some things really well, but in midfield you cannot afford to do anything really badly.

ball, giving him options, drawing defenders, even running from deep to become a striker himself. And of course he must support his fellow midfielders, because the midfield is the 'engine-room' of the team which makes things happen.

These days managers like to see – and indeed expect – their midfield men, or most of them, not only to be the architects of attacks but also to score goals as well.

So the midfielder requires it all – he must have limitless stamina and enthusiasm, as he covers most of the pitch, he must have pace, vision, ball control, a tackle and a shot.

A tall order! But no need to despair. As I mentioned earlier, there is a chance to specialise in midfield, as the tall Hoddle and the short Batty are quite different players. There are all

A tireless midfield ball-winner, David Batty also has the passing skills to set attacks going.

ADVANCED

SHOOTING SKILLS 1

There is nothing quite like the spectacle of a player volleying the ball into the back of the net from 25 yards. Imagine the thrill for the player who pulls it off in front of a packed house at Old Trafford, Elland Road, San Siro or some of the other big stadiums of the world!

The volleyed goal is always the most exciting and, as we are in the entertainment business, anything that excites the spectator has to be good for the game.

Players themselves get a thrill out of scoring with a volley and it is perhaps not surprising that this skill is one which most people seem to love to practise whether they are kids or professionals.

VOLLEYING

When French international striker Eric Cantona, determined to impress in English football, was playing with us at Leeds United he spent maybe ten or fifteen minutes every day after training practising volleying the ball at the goals. Eric's French international teammate Jean-Pierre Papin is another who puts time aside to practise the technique of volleying. Practice pays dividends

When a player volleys the ball he kicks it first time, before it has a chance to hit the ground. In other words he hits the ball while it is still in flight and, because you can swing the full weight of your body into this shot, the volley is regarded as the hardest or strongest method of striking the ball.

One of the most important considerations

is the position of the non-striking foot. At the time of impact you are standing on one foot only and the power you can get into the shot will depend on how well you have positioned yourself. This skill can come only with practice. A wall is a help, as you can throw the ball against it and practise volleying the ball back again. Soon you will find you instinctively take up the right position, and then you can practise volleying the ball at an angle as it comes from the wall.

To get the most power into the volley shot,

1 I have my eye firmly fixed on the ball, attempting to judge the pace of it as it comes towards me in the air and judging where to place my left foot.

you need to keep your toes pointing downwards and bring the upper part of your foot into contact with the moving ball.

The follow-through is not a long one, but you must not snatch at the ball – the volley must be executed smoothly, however quickly you have to move.

The principle of using the inside of the foot, as explained in Bending the Ball, can be used and, if the volley is struck accurately in this way, the ball will curve either to the left or right, depending on whether you have used the outside or inside of the foot.

3 I have swivelled my right hip around and, having kicked the ball, have followed through with the right leg.

2 Meeting the ball a couple of feet off the ground, I lean back away from the ball and prepare to kick it with the top of my foot.

Gordon's GEMS

● Timing is all important in this move so compose yourself as the ball flies through the air towards you.

● Do not take a wild swipe at the ball. Try to 'push' it through rather than take a stab at it.

● The ideal way to practise this move is to use a wall or have a friend throw the ball to you from a short distance.

ADVANCED SHOOTING SKILLS 2

THE HALF-VOLLEY

The half-volley is when you kick the ball a split second after it bounces. Like the volley, the half-volley can be used with power and is great to watch when executed successfully.

Making the half-volley is a relatively straightforward skill but a mistimed attempt can make the ball fly off in the wrong direction, so you must judge the flight of the ball correctly and time the kick perfectly.

Watch carefully the flight of the ball and estimate where it will bounce. Sometimes you have the choice of volleying or half-volleying. At other times the bounce will be too far away for you to reach the ball before it bounces, so the half-volley is a necessity.

Your non-kicking foot must be placed close to where the ball bounces, otherwise you will be stretching and off-balance. You bring your kicking leg through to meet the ball an inch or two after the bounce. Because the ball is actually rising as you hit it, the main fault is to sky the ball. Therefore you must get your head right over the ball. The third main requirement is to keep the toe pointing down. Keep your eye on the ball and follow through and you should make a satisfying shot.

Confidence is necessary to play the half-volley and confidence can come only with practice. The first things to acquire are control and accuracy. Our old friend the brick wall is a great help with practice. Throw or kick the ball against the wall and half-volley it as it comes back to you. Once you have learned to judge the ball correctly you can gradually add power to your kicking.

The half-volley can also be played softly as a pass, and the inside of the foot can be used as an alternative. This move can be practised conveniently by three players standing in a triangle, passing to each other on the half-volley.

The half-volley is also increasingly used by goalkeepers clearing from hand. The ball is more easily kept low with the half-volley or drop-kick compared to the more conventional punt.

1 The ball is about to bounce in front of me but just that bit too far away for me to hit it on the volley.

3 My right foot swings through but I keep my foot pointing downwards and forwards to keep the ball low. Notice I have my head firmly in position even though the ball has gone out of the photograph.

2 As the ball hits the ground, I have planted my left foot alongside it and I swing my kicking foot through to make contact using the instep immediately after the ball has struck the ground.

Gordon's GEMS

● Do not allow the ball to pitch too far in front of you.

● You can get 'swerve' on the half-volley shot if you use the outside of the foot following the instructions given in the earlier section on Bending the Ball.

● Never lean back when attempting the half-volley.

CROSSING THE BALL

I would estimate about 80 per cent of goals scored in football stem from crosses, so obviously this is a very important and productive part of the game. But there is more to crossing a ball than merely getting down the flank and whacking it into the middle in the hope that one of the forwards will be able to get to it.

It is no good crossing the ball when there is no one in the middle to receive it. That would be a waste of your own time and energy and, equally important, you would merely be giving possession of the ball to the opposition.

In situations like this, you need to be brave enough and to have sufficient confidence in your own ability to delay your move in the hope that a teammate will get into a forward position. If nobody is supporting you in the centre, then you must quickly decide on a different tactic, possibly cutting in with the ball to shoot yourself, or even winning a corner off a defender.

BYE-LINE CROSS

In the modern game, the cross that is played in quickly from the bye-line causes the most confusion to defenders.

Because they are running back they will be facing their own goal and unable to organise themselves or mark the strikers properly. As the strikers will be running in towards the ball, they have all the advantages. So the swiftly despatched cross – as opposed to the one where you check back onto your other foot and then cross – is the more dangerous.

The technique of crossing is important, of course, but the first thing to decide is where to put the ball. In the old days, the high cross to the far post was by far the most popular ball. The idea was to clear the goalkeeper for a powerful centre-forward like Tommy Lawton to put the

1 I have run with the ball to the perfect position for crossing it into the middle.

2 The ball has cleared the first defender, which is most important.

ball in. In recent years, the near-post cross for an onrushing striker to head powerfully, or for a striker to glance in or even head on further across goal is possibly even more productive.

When making the cross, you should endeavour to get your body facing the direction in which you will kick the ball. For instance, if you are cutting inside parallel with the bye-line, then you are kicking in the same direction you are running, and the cross is straightforward.

However, often you will be forced to cross at anything up to right angles to the direction of your run. The ball is travelling away from you, so the position of your non-kicking foot is vital. Balance is all-important, as the non-kicking foot must be close to the ball but at the same time leave room to swing the kicking foot.

If you are crossing from the right, the left foot should be behind and just inside the ball. With your arms spread to maintain balance, and your

eyes on the ball, bring your right foot down and across the ball, getting the inside of your foot under the ball to lift it across the goal. Keep the head down until the move is completed.

Gordon's GEMS

● You need good pace on the ball when making the cross into the middle.

● Always try to 'swerve' the ball away from the goalkeeper, making it difficult for him to collect.

3 I have delivered the ball in such a way that it is just too far out for the goalkeeper to collect.

4 This is the inch perfect cross, as the ball curls away from the goalkeeper, to be met by the on-rushing forward – and it's a goal!

HEADING THE BALL

Heading is vital in football, but it is a skill which young players are often not too anxious to learn. Perhaps they think it is not as glamorous as shooting hard or dribbling, but I have a feeling many youngsters fear that heading can be painful, particularly if they do not connect with the ball properly.

I am well aware that there will be readers who will wonder what I can teach them about heading, since it is well known that heading is not one of my strengths, to say the least. Well, short of getting Lee Chapman to write this section for me, all I can say is that I have played with some of the best headers in the game. There was Chapman, of course, and in the same Leeds United Championship-winning team, Gary Speed, Chris Whyte, Chris Fairclough and Mel Sterland, just to mention a few. So I know how it's done – even if I don't do it often myself!

The first thing to say is that, if you are a youngster, you might do well to practise at first with a light plastic ball. Once you are confident in your technique you will be able to transfer to a proper football knowing that you can head the ball competently and it will not hurt you.

The point of contact is the forehead – in other words that front part of your head between your eyebrows and your hairline. The skull here is much tougher than the ball, which will give an inch or two on impact, and you will find that you can soon make good headers without the ball hurting at all. Of course, to get the ball in the right place you must keep your eyes open! If you shut your eyes and hope, the ball will strike you rather than the other way round, and if it catches you in an awkward stance it could give you a headache.

The neck muscles also come into play when heading. You will have heard of players 'attacking' the ball and this is what you must do

1 Something of a collector's item – Gordon Strachan about to head the ball. I am leaning backwards in anticipation of using my neck muscles to thrust my head forward to meet the ball.

when heading. You must tense your neck muscles so that they are locked and supporting your head, and strike the ball positively, sending it in the direction you wish with conviction.

Heading the ball is less natural than kicking, and practice makes perfect. Throwing the ball against a wall so that it rebounds just above your head is a good way of practising alone. You can jump to head the ball back, remembering to thrust your head forward with a positive movement of the neck to get power behind the header. With a friend you can practise heading to each other, or with two friends you can play 'piggy in the middle'.

2 Hanging magnificently (!) in the air, with one leg slightly in front of the other, I have brought my head and the upper part of my body forward to get power into my header, and away the ball goes.

Gordon's GEMS

● Use your forehead to head the ball. You can get more power this way and be more accurate.

● Heading the ball does not hurt, so keep your eyes on the ball.

● Extend your arms to help give you balance when you are in the air.

● Make sure you judge the flight of the ball correctly.

TACKLING AND
WINNING THE BALL

Many people take tackling for granted but it really is an art in itself and something that you need to give plenty of attention to, and especially so if you are a defender. I have been trying it for 20 years - and on occasions actually in a game!

The real art of tackling is not merely to go in at an opponent but to come away with the ball after the tackle. My Leeds United teammate David Batty and Paul Ince of Manchester United are great exponents of tackling and winning the ball and well worth watching next time you get the chance.

1 Both myself and my opponent have an equal chance of getting the ball – it is what we call a 50-50 situation.

1 Here I am tracking an opponent who is in possession and running with the ball.

2 I am now close enough to my opponent and ready to slide in to the tackle and, I hope, win the ball.

3 Here I go, sliding in with my right foot going past the ball so that I can drag the ball back and win possession.

THE BLOCK TACKLE

More often than not I harrass and annoy opponents rather than use the block tackle and that is mainly because of my size. It would not be much use me attempting the block tackle on an opponent who is maybe three stones heavier than I am. I would more than likely lose out in the tackle.

The block tackle is used when two players go for the ball and arrive together, both putting their feet to the ball at the same time. When making the block tackle you should try to get your body weight over the top of the ball to add strength to your challenge.

2 We arrive at the ball at the same time. My foot is at one side of the ball and my opponent has one foot at the other side of it.

3 The stronger man wins and takes the ball away, having won possession for his side.

4 I've won the ball and I am about to get to my feet quickly and move away from my opponent, who cannot recover so quickly.

THE SLIDE TACKLE

There is more to this manoeuvre than just sliding into an opponent. When you slide in, try to make sure you get your foot round the ball and then get to your feet as quickly as possible to be ready to move away with the ball.

Key elements in this tackle are surprise and determination but timing is all important as well. Usually you are coming in from the side or behind as you make this tackle and if your timing is not right you are likely to give away a free kick and that can spell danger for your side.

Newcastle's Peter Beardsley is probably the best at this particular tackle. He's magnificent, in fact, because he times it so well and almost always comes away with the ball.

CLOSING DOWN YOUR OPPONENT

Hard work is the key to the success of this manoeuvre and, having been with Leeds United when we fought a season-long, energy-sapping battle with Manchester United and won the League Championship in 1991-92, I know all about this particular aspect of the game.

Closing down and pressurising opponents is not the most glamourous part of the game but it is a necessary part and calls for a great deal of hard work by every member of the team. Tommy Craig, Celtic's assistant manager, told me he regarded Leeds United as having been the hardest working team in Britain in our title winning season.

Basically, closing down the opposition means giving the man with the ball as little time and space as possible to play it, and marking his teammates closely so that he has no easy option for a pass. Sooner or later the player on the ball will become frustrated and take a risk – and your team gets a chance to gain possession.

The plan, however, will not work effectively if one or two members of your team suddenly feel they are tired and ease off. It takes a united effort from the team as a whole to make it successful and, as we at Leeds showed in our title-winning season, it can be a very effective plan.

It stops the opposition from playing and allows you greater opportunity to display your attacking skills. Basically, what you have to do is make sure you mark the defender closest to you but the plan as a whole is helped if players shout instructions and encouragement to each other – it is very much a team effort.

One of the hardest working teams over the years has undoubtedly been Liverpool. Ian Rush and John Barnes have been two of the greatest strikers in the game but they have frequently come back to close people down in midfield and catch people in possession. Their work rate has been phenomenal.

Peter Bearsdley is another who works very hard to catch people in possession, as I know to my cost and embarrassment. During Leeds United's Premier League game against Everton at Goodison Park in the 1992-93 season he caught me in possession, took the ball away from me and crossed for Tony Cottee to score.

Gordon's GEMS

● Don't worry about hard work. If you do plenty of it, it will become a habit and you won't feel it.

● Shout encouragement to teammates, especially if they show signs of tiredness.

● Remember, the quicker you win back the ball the quicker you can score a goal.

● Try to stay on your feet at all times to keep up the pressure on an opponent.

1 I notice the player in possession is looking to pass to his teammate on the wing.

2 By moving in to challenge I have successfully cut off the ground pass to his teammate.

3 Having stopped the move, I run in to close my opponent down and try to win possession.

TAKING A THROW-IN 1

Ten years ago the aim of the throw-in was to try to keep possession. But in today's game the throw-in can also lead directly from one throw to a goal so it has become a very important part of the game in an attacking sense.

There are three different types of throw-in – the long, the short and the quick.

The short throw and the quick throw are basically to get the ball back in play on the ground and then to keep possession and to go on and make a goalscoring opportunity.

The long throw is used, in the main, anywhere within say 30 yards from the goal line in the attacking area. Believe it or not, we now have some teams in British football who actually play to get a throw-in from that kind of distance. No, I'm not kidding!

Some teams are fortunate to have players who can make a long throw into the penalty area, so that the throw-in becomes almost as effective a set-piece as a corner. Otherwise, if they are too far out to be able to throw the ball into the goalmouth, a quick throw to a colleague to play the ball first time into the centre is used. In either case, a dangerous cross results from the throw.

However, I would say to any young player that playing for position for a long throw-in is not the way to go about playing football. But as a weapon, the long throw-in is a valuable one. Obviously you need someone in your side who is big and strong, though I cannot see anyone at Under 10 level managing to throw the ball to the front post. So for younger footballers, and smaller players such as myself, the short and quick throws are the ones for us.

1 The throw is about to be taken and I move to my left, taking my marker with me.

2 I have switched directions and am about to lose my marker.

58

LOSING YOUR MARKER

Never stand rooted to the spot when waiting for a teammate to take a throw-in because you will give your marker a much better chance of nipping in to take up possession.

Movement is the key to throwing off the unwanted attentions of an opponent. As the throw-in is about to be taken, move as though you are going to run in one direction and then switch quickly to go in another.

By doing this you will have a chance of wrong footing your opponent and taking up possession from the throw-in.

Gordon's GEMS

● Move around to outwit defenders. Even if you don't get the ball, you could create space for colleagues.

● Be aware of what defenders are doing behind you as a throw-in is about to be taken.

● Keep an eye open for the quick throw-in. It can often catch the opposition off their guard.

3 My teammate begins a dummy run as the ball is thrown towards me.

4 Here I am free of all opposition and about to take up possession from the throw-in.

THROWING IN CORRECTLY

It is very easy to lose concentration at a throw-in. It is surprising how many players see the throw-in merely as a routine method of getting the ball back in play, in spite of the possibility of a goal resulting from the throw.

However, at the worst, a throw-in awarded to your side should be a way to ensure that your side keeps possession. And when you consider that any team can expect to take between 20 and 50 throw-ins in a match, you can see the importance of taking care and executing the throw well.

The worst thing you can do when taking a throw-in is to lose possession. And if you forget the basics and lose your concentration, you stand a good chance of making a mess of things.

So the first thing to remember is to concentrate. When making the throw, keep both feet firmly on the ground and behind the touchline as you lift your arms above your head.

It may sound unnecessary for me to be explaining this but, even at the top professional level, players still manage to make a foul throw. They are guilty of handing the ball to their opponents, which is a stupid thing to do.

So when you take a throw, concentrate first on getting the mechanics right. And do not just throw the ball in the general direction of a teammate.

1 I'm taking a quick throw-in but my attacking partner is flat-footed, which shows he is not mentally sharp. We are both at fault – particularly me for throwing the ball at that time.

2 The ball has pitched a couple of feet in front of my teammate, which makes it difficult for him to control it quickly.

Try to make the ball reach him without bouncing. It is much easier for him to control the ball if it comes straight to his head or his foot. If it bounces a yard or so in front of him it is not as easy for him to bring the ball under control quickly and a defender is therefore allowed a little more time to intercept the ball or dispossess him.

Do not throw the ball to the side of a teammate if there is a defender close-marking him on that side. It gives the defender a chance to stretch round and steal the ball.

You cut down the risk of your team losing possession if the player receiving the ball plays it back to you first time. If your teammate can do that, then I reckon you have taken a good throw-in.

Gordon's GEMS

● It is not necessary to throw the ball as far as you can. A short throw-in can be just as effective.

● Think of a throw as making a pass with your hands – there is no real excuse for not being accurate.

● As you pick up the ball, look around to see if you can catch the opposition off guard with a quickly taken throw.

3 The ball bounces into his midriff and he is going to need more touches than he might like before he can get the ball under control.

4 He now has to play the ball with his left foot and, as that is the side the defender is on, there is more chance of him losing possession.

TAKING PENALTIES 1

Penalty taking is all about being confident and, if you do not feel happy about taking one, then the short answer to that is – don't try it!

Games can be won and lost on penalty kicks so you should be in the right frame of mind – positive and confident – when taking one.

A SHORT RUN-UP

This is a spot kick I have used on rare occasions and when it comes off it is great – but you can look very foolish if it fails.

You must have the confidence to attempt this move quickly as the idea is to catch the keeper off his guard.

The short run-up began in Italy where goalkeepers were getting away with moving early and coming off their line. With the quickly taken penalty, the keeper has less chance of moving. He may even be caught unprepared as you place the ball down, take a couple of paces back and fire the ball into the net. But you must hit the ball with sufficient pace and aim for one of the corners.

'PLACED' PENALTY

I have no wish to boast, but over the years I have managed to be quite successful at taking penalties and the placed shot is the one I prefer.

It has brought me the majority of my spot kick successes and from a general point of view I think this is the most popular and widely used method of trying to score from the penalty spot.

1 Only after I have relaxed for a moment to concentrate on building up my confidence do I begin my run towards the ball.

1 I have taken a couple of steps backwards and I'm about to step forward quickly to take aim.

2 Making contact with the ball, I have aimed for the stanchion inside the left-hand corner of the goal.

Few players have a harder shot on them than Leeds United's Scottish international Gary McAllister, yet even he prefers to take a placed penalty rather than the kicking the ball as hard as he can.

When attempting the placed penalty it is essential that you are confident and positive. I find you have greater control and accuracy if you use the inside of the foot.

The goalkeeper will do his best to put you off, but concentrate on what you are going to do and just before you run to the ball, glance at the corner of the goal in which you are *not* planning to put the ball and with a bit of luck the keeper might decide to dive that way, as you place the ball into the opposite corner.

Another way of deceiving him is to make it look as though you are aiming, say, for the right-hand corner of the goal and then to drop your shoulders and place the ball into the opposite corner.

In the top professional leagues these days penalty taking is more difficult than it was because goalkeepers now have more knowledge of players who usually take penalties.

This is down to television coverage, and any goalkeeper worth his salt will have videos of penalties being taken by different players and will study them to see just which side a player prefers to place his penalties. But this will not, of course, be the case in amateur leagues, so the best of luck, all you budding penalty kings!

2 I make it look as though I am going to aim the ball just inside the goalkeeper's left-hand post making him tense himself to dive that way.

3 At the last second I change direction and with the inside of the foot kick the ball to the keeper's right, sending him the wrong way.

3 The ball is on its way into the left-hand corner of the net and the keeper has been caught by surprise.

4 The keeper has hardly moved and can only watch as the ball hits the back of the net. Another penalty success for me!

TAKING PENALTIES 2

THE BLASTED PENALTY

The penalty kick that is blasted towards goal is one I do not particularly care for. The reason is that I feel the penalty taker loses some accuracy when concentrating solely on power and this allows the goalkeeper a better chance.

Whenever the blasted penalty is mentioned, my mind goes back to a match between Manchester United and Everton. I had been the United penalty taker but having missed three of my last four the manager Ron Atkinson decided that if any penalty award was to come our way Jesper Olsen would take it.

It was a great relief going out for the game knowing that, should we be awarded a spot kick, I would not have to take it. I could concentrate on my game. However, after only a few minutes

Olsen himself was brought down and we were awarded a penalty. Having just been heavily tackled Jesper felt he was not able to take the spot kick himself!

I glanced at my other teammates and they all seemed to be looking towards our own goalkeeper, Gary Bailey. They obviously were not too interested in taking the kick, and as I was the only one looking towards Neville Southall, I picked up the ball and placed it on the spot.

So there I was, facing the best goalkeeper in the world and in front of a 58,000 crowd. Because I had not had much success in recent weeks with penalties I decided to change my style and blast this one. As I ran up, I made the mistake of looking up to see where Southall was and when I aimed my kick I scuffed the ground and sent a piece of turf flying into the net while the ball rolled so gently towards the goal that Southall had to move forward to pick it up.

Needless to say, that was the end of my

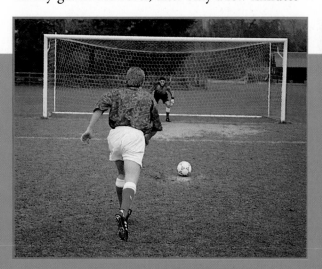

1 Having made up my mind what part of the goal I am going to put the ball into I make my run towards the ball.

2 Contact has been made with the ball and I have put everything into the shot to give the ball plenty of pace.

penalty taking days at Old Trafford!

However, this type of penalty does produce the goods provided it is executed correctly. In my experience, no one was better at it than Francis Lee, who held a great record for penalties at Bolton Wanderers, Manchester City and Derby County in the 1960s and early 1970s.

The secret of success with the fiercely struck penalty kick is to make up your mind where you are going to put the ball and then keep your eyes on the ball when you take the kick. Do not look at the goalkeeper and remember to follow through with the kicking leg.

All the spectators, if any, plus the other players, will be watching intently when you take a penalty. Shut them all out of your mind and concentrate solely on the task of scoring.

Confidence is of the essence with a spot kick. My confidence had suffered quite badly before I took that penalty against Everton and failed. Confidence comes with practice, of course, and

fortunately practising penalties is quite easy, particularly if you have a goalkeeping friend who wants to practise stopping them!

Gordon's GEMS

- Decide where you are going to hit the ball and don't let anything put you off. Go for it.

- Do not change your mind when you are running up to kick the ball.

- Keep your eye on the ball and make sure you are well over the ball when you make contact.

3 I have made sure that my kicking leg has followed through. This is essential if you are to give the ball pace.

4 The goalkeeper has chosen the correct side to dive but because of the pace of the ball he is beaten and it is a goal.

CURLING ROUND THE WALL

I explained earlier in the book how to 'bend' or 'curl' the ball. If you studied that section and worked on the movement you will be able to curl free kicks round a defensive wall in matches.

Mastering the art of bending a ball takes a lot of practice, and when you are young you will not find this skill quite as easy to acquire as the player who is older and stronger. Nevertheless, if you can develop this ability at an early age it will stand you in good stead later when there will be more opportunity to put it to use in matches.

At Leeds United we prided ourselves on the strength of our defensive wall and I don't think we conceded more than one or two goals in our Championship winning season of 1991-92 from a shot curled round our wall. That was because we had a wall comprised of many big and brave players well organised by our keeper, John Lukic.

I doubt whether we would have been as successful with this defensive tactic had we been playing in the Italian or Brazilian league. In those leagues the curling free kick seems to be easier to perfect, and teams often have two or three people who are adept at it. Defences are therefore more prepared for it and better skilled at countering it.

Curling the ball does not just happen naturally – a lot of practice is required. Because of the climate in countries like Brazil or Italy it is far easier for players to stay behind after an afternoon's play to practise.

In Britain, however, we do not have so many sunny days and it is very hard to come back for

1 Having picked my spot, I am about to strike the ball with the inside of my foot.

2 The ball is played a couple of feet outside the post and I follow through with my kicking leg.

extra training in the pouring rain. Trying to curl the ball for half an hour or more in ankle-deep mud is not everyone's idea of fun. But the value of this skill has been shown often in recent years by such as Diego Maradona and Roberto Baggio, two great exponents of the art.

For curling the ball, allied to sheer brute force to send the ball round a wall, you will not see a better exponent than England and Nottingham Forest defender Stuart Pearce. He scored with a brilliant curling free kick against Tottenham in the 1991/92 FA Cup final. It was curled round the wall at a very fast pace and in my view was one of the best free kicks you will ever see. Manchester United's young Welsh international Ryan Giggs is another player who skilfully demonstrates the art of curling the ball.

Combining power with curl is difficult, as you are making contact with the outside of the ball, rather than striking firmly through the centre. Power comes from increasing the speed of the foot, from following through forcefully, and from the angle of the foot. The more upright the foot as it kicks the ball, the more power can go into the kick.

The players I have mentioned are all world class, but don't let that put you off having a go yourself. If you can be bothered to put the time in working at this move, and have determination and confidence, there is no reason why you should not become proficient in it.

Off the pitch, you can practise the skill by using a dustbin or some other obstacle as the 'wall'. When you come to use it in a game, my advice is to aim the ball a couple of feet outside the goal post and, if you have kicked the ball as it should be kicked, the 'curl' will bring it back on target for goal.

3 The ball has now 'curled' back and is going into the net Just underneath the bar.

TAKING FREE KICKS 2

ADDING MEN TO THE WALL

Adding attackers to a defensive wall has been a classic move for Nottingham Forest. Over the years I would think they have scored more goals than any other team in England as a result of putting their own men into the wall of defenders.

They line up one or two men on the end of the wall. When Steve Hodge was at the club he was always the one closest to the wall and, as Stuart Pearce took the free kick, he could push against the wall while the Forest player on the outside edge of the wall would peel away leaving a gap for the ball to go through. However, be careful not to be drawn into a barging match with defenders. Your team has a chance to score

– don't encourage the ref to blow up against you.

It is a ploy that works well, especially if you have someone who can hit the ball as hard and accurately as Pearce. The goalkeeper does not see the ball until late and often there is no time for him to make a save.

MAN UTD v SPURS 1986-87

I run over the ball (see diagram opposite) and past the Spurs wall. Bryan Robson plays the ball to Jesper Olsen who then plays it into my path. I play it first time across the six yard box to Norman Whiteside who scores.

1 The defenders are lined up to protect the right half of the goal and we add two attackers to the left side of the 'wall to hinder the goalkeeper's view.

2 A gap is created as one attacker peels away and the other pushes into the defenders in the wall.

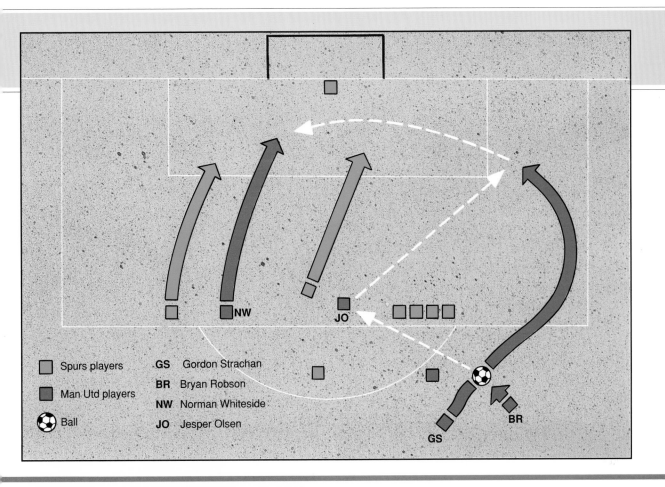

Spurs players

Man Utd players

⚽ Ball

GS Gordon Strachan
BR Bryan Robson
NW Norman Whiteside
JO Jesper Olsen

3 The ball is through and on its way to the goal, leaving the keeper with a hard task.

Gordon's GEMS

● If you are an attacker on the end of a wall you should remember to be alert at all times.

● Leave it as late as you can before peeling away, so that the ball is kept from the goalkeeper's view as long as possible.

● If you are taking the free kick, put plenty of pace on the ball – and be accurate.

TAKING CORNERS 1

Corner kicks were an important and very productive part of Leeds United's armoury when we won the League Championship in 1991-92. Near post corners, back post corners, short corners – you name them and we got the best out of them.

Being on the short side and therefore not able to get many penalty area headers in, I have taken corners all along for Leeds but we were lucky in that we had other players who could take accurate corners, either curling them in or out, in Tony Dorigo and Gary McAllister.

Accuracy is of paramount importance if you are to make the most of corner kicks. The kicker has to be able to pick out teammates either at the near post or the back post, otherwise the defending team have a much easier chance of clearing the danger.

THE NEAR POST CORNER

I find the near post corner is a particularly dangerous one. It is difficult to defend against if you have the right men to execute the move.

If you station a couple of big men at the near post and aim the ball to them, it is very difficult

1 I have taken the corner kick and the ball is on its way towards the near post.

2 My two teammates waiting at the near post watch closely as the ball drops towards them.

for the goalkeeper to come and collect the ball. These men should be strong and have good control with their heads. The idea is to hit one of your own men at the near post and for him to flick the ball on with his head.

That is the first part of the operation. Once you have got a successful flick on at the near post, you need a player who is fearless and athletic flying in at the back post. You need someone who sees nothing but the ball and goes for it without thinking about his personal safety.

For me the perfect example of this type of player is Arsenal's Tony Adams. As far as Leeds United are concerned, Chris Fairclough did a similar job well.

Practising near post corner kicks can become boring but, when you pull one off in a game and it leads to a goal, you get a tremendous feeling of satisfaction.

Taking advantage of your set pieces goes a long way towards winning games.

3 One of my attacking teammates, who is blocking the path of the goalkeeper, gets the first flick on with his head.

4 Seeing the ball flicked on, another attacking player comes in at the back post to head the ball. (On this occasion, however, it has gone over the bar!)

FAR POST CORNER

This is the basic corner kick and is used when you believe that your best header of the ball can beat the opposing team's best header of the ball.

It is important to have players at the front post, in order to keep the defence guessing and to block the goalkeeper's view and make it more difficult for him to come off his line and intercept the ball. Manchester United's Denis Irwin and Gary Pallister play this corner as well as any pair I have seen.

Pallister likes a high curling ball played into the penalty area where he can use his own height to the best advantage. He is probably the best in the country at the far post corner, aided, of course, by accurately delivered crosses from teammate Irwin.

Movement before the kick is very important if you are the striker. It gives the taker of the kick a signal of your intention and helps him aim the kick towards you. It also helps you to lose your marker. Always be on your toes to avoid your marker getting too close to you.

It is not too often that goals are scored at the far post by headers direct from the corner kick but there is always the chance of a knock down to cause havoc in the defence so that other players might be able to pinch a goal.

THE QUICKLY TAKEN CORNER

1 My side have won a corner and, as I make my way to the corner, I look round to see whether I can take the kick quickly.

2 A teammate is alert to my thinking and I immediately aim the ball towards him.

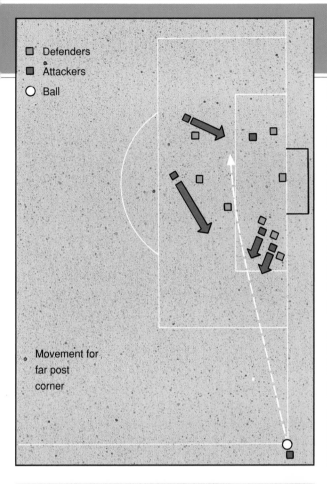

Defenders
Attackers
Ball

Movement for
far post
corner

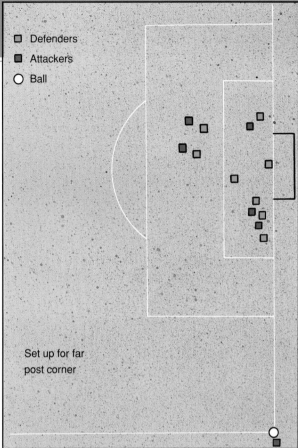

Defenders
Attackers
Ball

Set up for far
post corner

3 He has come towards me to meet the ball and quickly plays it back to me.

4 In turn, I hit the ball low into the six yard area where another teammate is waiting.

PLAYING IN DEFENCE

Many managers will tell you that if you are building a successful side you begin first of all with the defence. I am not about to argue with that belief.

Defence is a very important part of any side and I do not intend to be derogatory in any way to Arsenal when I say that over the past five years the mainstay of their success has been the defence. Its great strength has been its organisation as a unit, but as individuals the Arsenal defenders take a great pride in their

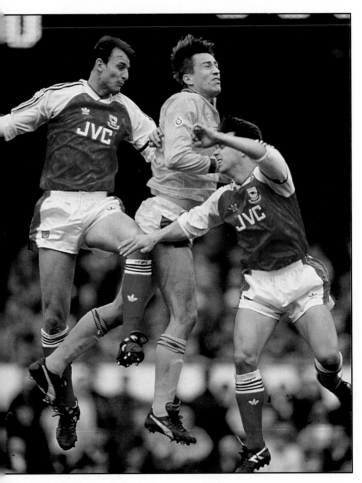

My teammate Lee Chapman struggles to make an impression against Arsenal's Steve Bould and David Hillier.

record, and one obvious thing about their play is the enjoyment they derive from defending. They take pleasure in being miserly in not allowing you many shots at goal and they make you work very hard for the few you might manage.

Technically, as individuals they are not, perhaps, the most gifted of players. But they display the same high standards week in and week out, which must be very reassuring for manager George Graham. Consistency is the keynote.

The main job of a central defender is to prevent goals. This might sound obvious, but what I want to emphasise is the secondary nature of everything else. A tall central defender who scores occasionally from set pieces is valuable, but he is no good if he also concedes goals.

If you play central defender, remember the simple thing is always best. Get the ball away, even if you concede a corner or throw-in. Do not over-elaborate or be too ambitious. Doing the unexpected might bamboozle the opposition but it might also confuse your colleagues, and confusion is the last thing you want in your own penalty area.

Full-backs must also give priority to their defensive duties, which include covering for the central defenders. But a full-back often has a particular opponent to mark – the opposition's wide striker on his side of the pitch. He must make sure his opponent gets as little of the ball as possible, so the full-back must be able to read the game accurately.

But these days a full-back is also expected to become a wide attacker at times. He is often the man who can by-pass the midfield and get deep into opposition territory to get across telling centres. So if you play full-back you must be mobile, fast and able to cross the ball.

All the defenders must be able to tackle, so

One of the greatest defenders in world football is Paolo Maldini of Italian champions AC Milan. Pace, anticipation and determination make him an outstanding opponent.

practise this skill. But a tackler must also learn discretion. The worst thing you can do is to commit yourself to the tackle and be beaten, thus giving your colleagues an extra man to contend with while you are out of play.

As mentioned earlier, defending is a team operation, so the best you can do for your team-mates is to keep goalside of your opponent, denying him a clear run at goal. When he is in possession, try to jockey him into positions where he cannot be dangerous. Restrict his space.

To be a successful defender you must develop a good understanding with your fellow defenders. The more you play together the better the understanding should become. Knowing what your fellow defenders are capable of, what they are likely to do and where they will be, is the key to this success.

Another important ingredient is communication. Players who shout instructions on the pitch are a great help. David Seaman and Tony Adams of Arsenal are the two best in the country at this. Adams never seems to stop talking which must be reassuring for the other defenders.

Try to size up the situation when you haven't got the ball and if you think you can assist a teammate by shouting an instruction to him then do so. It might be a case of simply warning him of a likely challenge, or it may be to tell him to pass the ball to a certain player.

When the high ball is coming at you and you feel you are in a better position to deal with it than a fellow defender, shout and let him know that. You will then avoid having two men going for the same ball.

Football is a TEAM game and you will be a better player if you remember that.

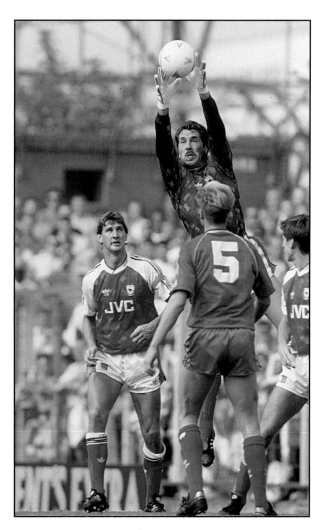

Two more reasons why Arsenal have one of the Premier League's outstanding defences – England's David Seaman and Tony Adams.

75

GORDON'S BEST TEAM

I have selected two best teams – one of players I have played with and one of players I have played against. My selections were made on the strength of players' performances and ability at the time I played with or against them.

Kenny Dalglish was the best I ever played with or against in British football.

MY BEST TEAMMATES XI

GOALKEEPER
Jim Leighton (*Aberdeen*)

BACK FOUR
Stuart Kennedy (*Aberdeen*)
Paul McGrath (*Manchester United*)
Willie Miller (*Aberdeen*)
Tony Dorigo (*Leeds United*)

MIDFIELD
Gary McAllister (*Leeds United*)
Bryan Robson (*Manchester United*)
Norman Whiteside (*Manchester United*)

FORWARDS
Mark Hughes (*Manchester United*)
Mark McGhee (*Aberdeen*)
Peter Weir (*Aberdeen*)

SUB
Gary Speed (*Leeds United*)

I suspect right at the outset that I will have raised a few eyebrows by going for goalkeeper Jim Leighton and for Peter Weir in the forwards.

Peter, who played at Aberdeen, will not, perhaps, be known to many people but I think between 1981 and 1984 he was probably the best wide player in Britain. He was also the best two-footed player I have played with.

Jim may have found it difficult when he came to England, but when I played with him in Scotland he was phenomenal.

Norman Whiteside and Bryan Robson were simply magnificent in midfield for Manchester United in my time there. Although Whiteside had barely turned 21, he was unbelievable. Switching from the role of striker to midfield was no problem for this player who had such vision and ability.

The ability of players of today such as my Leeds United teammates Tony Dorigo and Gary McAllister, and Paul McGrath and Mark Hughes really speaks for itself.

No one beat Stuart Kennedy. That summed him up perfectly. He was tough and arrogant and if I backtracked with the idea of helping him he would tell me to get lost. I am sure he took it personally if anyone even tried to get past him.

Mark McGhee was totally unpredictable but totally committed to his game, being strong and brave and he scored a lot of goals, while Willie Miller was simply the best leader I have ever played with.

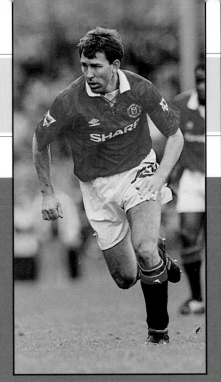

Bryan Robson's strength and courage were an inspiration in my United days.

It would be difficult to think of a more difficult marking job than Diego Maradona. Remember his second goal against England in the '86 World Cup?

Taking on Franco Baresi would be most forwards' worst nightmare!

BEST OPPOSITION XI

GOALKEEPER
Pat Jennings (*Northern Ireland*)

BACK FOUR
Manuel Amoros (*France*)
Franco Baresi (*Italy*)
Alan Hansen (*Scotland*)
Paolo Maldini (*Italy*)

MIDFIELD
Michel Platini (*France*)
Toninho Cerezo (*Brazil*)

FORWARDS
Chris Waddle (*England*)
Marco Van Basten (*Holland*)
Diego Maradona (*Argentina*)
Kenny Dalglish (*Scotland*)

Mostly, I suppose, we think of Brazilians as ball playing wizards but Cerezo was the hard working man in midfield who could make runs for other people. A wonderful player.

The pure ability displayed by the likes of Michel Platini (who was unsuspectingly quick), Maradona and Marco Van Basten make them obvious choices in my book – truly great players in every sense of the word and I suppose few would argue otherwise.

From what I have seen in British football Kenny Dalglish was the best of the lot. I don't go back as far as the likes of Stanley Matthews or Tom Finney but as far as I am concerned Kenny had everything. I also have great admiration for the skills of Chris Waddle.

So far as the defenders are concerned, the Italians, Franco Baresi and Paolo Maldini, Manuel Amoros of France and Scotland's Alan Hansen make up my perfect back four in front of goalkeeper Pat Jennings.

PREPARATION AND ATTITUDE

Having the right kind of preparation for matches is, of course, vital for professional footballers but it is also important for those who play the game as amateurs and, indeed, at youth and schoolboy level.

When you are a youngster you will probably have the right kind of preparation because parents usually insist that children get to bed early anyway because of school. So you should be in good shape.

Anyone under the age of 14 should not really have too much of a problem because of the lifestyle they lead up to that age. As you get older you should begin to prepare yourself, as games will be getting harder, there will be a lot more running involved and it is bound to be much more physical.

DIET

Remember to treat your body as an engine and put the right petrol in. If you put the wrong stuff in, it will break down. If you put diesel into a four-star engine you will not get the best of results! The body's petrol is food.

So take care to look after your body with proper rest and diet before games. Get enough rest and sleep the night before a match and do not eat too much before playing. My diet as a footballer is, perhaps, well known because it has received a lot of publicity in newspapers in recent years. Though it is ideal for me as a professional footballer, I suppose it could easily be adapted for amateurs or schoolboys.

I start out in the morning by eating a bowl of porridge, made with milk, and with bananas mixed in. Believe it or not, most people who have tried it, like it!

At lunch time, before a game, I have a bowl of fresh fruit salad, though sometimes, during the coldest of the winter months, I will have a poached egg on toast. On the day before a game I eat pasta but without sauce. Plain pasta with a bit of butter on it is the order of the day for me.

During the week my diet usually consists of porridge and bananas in a morning, a piece of toast at lunch time, and meat – usually chicken – and pasta at night.

I eat a lot of pasta, which gives me plenty of energy. Putting on weight is not a problem if I am doing a lot of running because I burn off the energy it gives me. In summer, when I am not playing, I stay off the pasta.

I also take seaweed tablets. Seaweed is a natural substance, rather than buying vitamins. Seaweed has all the vitamins you need. It does not make me a more skilful player but I'm a great swimmer!

Gone are the days, I'm afraid, when players were told to eat steak. When I was a youngster at Dundee I used to love pre-match meals because, living in digs all week, the pre-match meal was probably the best meal of the week and I used to over-indulge in the steak, even though it was only about three hours before a game. But that sort of thing is just not on these days.

REST

I am lucky in that, as a professional, I can get to my bed on a couple of afternoons a week. I know it is a bit more difficult for amateurs but if you

confident of winning.

One thing you have to remember, however, is that you cannot guarantee to yourself, your manger or your teammates that you are going to play well in every game. No one can, no matter who he is.

If you don't play well, then fair enough, but you can still win if you have given 100 per cent effort. It is easier to sit down after a game and face your teammates, or your manager, if you know you have given everything you can and tried your hardest.

Years ago I used to get very upset if I did not play well but the assistant manager at Aberdeen told me that the only thing you can guarantee is trying all the time. That is something I have never forgotten.

FITNESS

I have not mentioned in this section on preparation the need to keep physically fit and to practise. This is because I hope these requirements are obvious.

Nobody can play football seriously if he is not fit, and I have emphasised throughout this book the need to practise. Let me assure you again that I still practise, even after 20 years in the top flight.

In this book, I hope I have sufficiently stressed the importance of play together as a team. If you start doing things for yourself in a game, then the time has come for you to think again. You must always play for the team, not yourself.

are a serious player then you should look to get some decent sleep at night I try to get my best sleep – and usually succeed – on a Thursday night before a Saturday game. I am not against players staying up late on Friday nights as long as they are relaxing.

MENTAL PREPARATION

When kick-off time is approaching it is important that you are in the right frame of mind for the game – and that means being

INDEX

Page numbers in italic denote
illustrations

Aberdeen 8, 9, 19, 20, 76
Adams, Tony 71, 75, *75*
Advanced shooting skills 46-
    9, *46, 47, 48, 49*
Amoros, Manuel 77
Arsenal *9*, 30, 71, 74,
    74, 75, *75*
Aston Villa 36
Atkinson, Ron 26-7, 36, 64
Attacking 26-7
Attitude 78, 79

Baggio, Roberto 67
Bailey, Gary 64
Bananas 78
Baresi, Franco 77, *77*
Barnes, John 56
Batty, David 44, 45, *45*, 54
Beardsley, Peter 55, 56
Beating your opponent 38-43,
    38, 39, 40, 41, 42, 43
Bending round the wall 66,
    66, 67
Bending the ball 16, *16, 17*, 47
Best, George 39, 40
Blackburn Rovers *27*
Blackpool 39
"Blasted" penalties 64-5, *64, 65*
Block tackle 55, *55*
Bolton Wanderers 39, 65
Bould, Steve *74*
Brazil 36, *44*, 77
Bruce, Steve 23, 24
Bye-line cross 50-51, *50, 51*

Cantona, Eric 46
Celtic 56
Cerezo, Toninho *44*, 77
Chapman, Lee 52, *74*
Chipped pass 14, *14, 15*
Chipping keeper 32-3, *32, 33*
Close control 34-7, *35, 37*
Close-range shooting 28-9,
    28, 29
Closing down opponents 56, *57*
Controlling on chest 22, *22*
Controlling on thigh 23, *23*
Controlling with head 24
Controlling with inside of
    leg 21, *21*
Corners 70-3, *70, 71, 72, 73*
Cottee, Tony 56
Craig, Tommy 56
Crossing the ball 50-51, *50, 51*
Cruyff, Johann 42, 43
"Cruyff turn", the 36, 42-3,
    42, 43

Curling round the wall 66,
    66, 67
Curling the ball 16, *16, 17*, 47
Cut away 34, *35*
Cut, the 40-41, *41*

Dalglish, Kenny 12, 40, *76*, 77
Defending 74-5
Derby County 65
Diet 78
Dorigo, Tony 70, 76
Dribbling 34, *35*
Driving through the wall 66, 67
Dummying over the ball 36,
    37
Dundee 8, 18, 19, 29, 78

England 26, 67, 77, *77*
Everton 56, 64, 65

Fairclough, Chris 52, 71
Far post corners 72
Ferguson, Alex 20, 24
Finland 9
Finney, Tom 77
First touch 20-25, *20, 21,
    22, 23, 24, 25*
Fitness 79
France 46, 77
Francis, Trevor 43
Fruit salad 78

Giggs, Ryan 67
Graham, George 74
Grobbelaar, Bruce 33

Half-volley 48, *48, 49, 49*
Hansen, Alan 33, 77
Harford, Mick 26, *26*
Heading the ball 52-3, *52, 53*
Hillier, David *9*, 74
Hoddle, Glenn 12, 44, 45, *45*
Hodge, Steve 68
Holland *27*, 42, 77
Hughes, Mark 76

Ince, Paul 54
Inside of foot 10, 11, *11*
Instep 10, *10*, 11, *11*
Irwin, Denis 72
Italy 77

Jennings, Pat 77
Johnstone, Jimmy 40

Kennedy, Stuart 76
Kicking 10-11, *10*
Kilmarnock 19

Lawton, Tommy 50

Lee, Francis 65
Leeds United 8, *8*, 9, *9*, 24,
    30, 44, *45*, 52, 54, 56, 63,
    66, 70, 71, 76
Leighton, Jim 76
Lineker, Gary 26, 29
Liverpool *9*, 33, 56
Long throw-in 58
Long-range shooting 30-31, *31*
Losing your marker *58*, 59, *59*
Lukic, John 66

Maldini, Paolo *75*, 77
Manchester City 40, 65
Manchester United 8, 9, *9*, 20,
    23, 24, 33, 44, 54, 56,
    64, 67, 68, *69*, 72, 76
Maradona, Diego 67, 77, *77*
Matthews, Stanley 38, 39, 77
"Matthews", the 38-9, *38, 39*
McAllister, Gary 20, 63, 70, 76
McGhee, Mark 76
McGrath, Paul 76
McNab, Neil 40
Mental preparation 79
Midfield play 44-5
Milan *75*
Milk 78
Miller, Willie 76

Near post corners 70-1, *70, 71*
Nevin, Pat 40
Newcastle United 55
Northern Ireland 9
Nottingham Forest 67, 68

Olsen, Jesper 64, 68, *69*
One-on-one 33
Outside of foot 10, 11, *11*

Pallister, Gary 24, 72
Papin, Jean-Pierre 46
Passing 12-19, *12, 13, 14,
    15, 16, 17, 18, 19*
Passing with head 24, *25*
Pasta and butter 78
Pearce, Stuart 67, 68
Pele 42
Penalties 62-5, *62, 63, 64, 65*
"Placed" penalties 62-3, *62, 63*
Platini, Michel 77
Poached egg 78
Porridge 78
Preparation 78, 79

Quick throw-in 58
Quickly taken corners *72, 73*
Rivelino 36
Robson, Bryan 44, 68, *69*, 76,
    77

Romania *32*
Rush, Ian 26, 56

Scotland 8, 9, *9*, *32*, 42, 63, 76
Scott, Jocky 18
Seaman, David 75, *75*
Seaweed tablets 78
Shearer, Alan 26, *27*
Sheffield Wednesday 43
Shooting at goal 28-33, *28,
    29, 30, 31, 32, 33*
Short run-up for penalties
    62, *62, 63*
Short throw-in 58
Sidefoot pass 13, *12, 13*
Slide tackle 55, *55*
Souness, Graeme 12
Southall, Neville 64
Speed, Gary 24, 52, 76
Steak 78
Sterland, Mel 52
Steven, Trevor 27

Tackling 54-5, *54, 55*
Taking free kicks 66-9, *66,
    67, 68, 69*
Throw-ins 58-61, *58, 59, 60, 61*
Throwing in correctly 60-61,
    60, 61
Toast 78
Top of foot 11, *11*
Tottenham Hotspur 67, 68, *69*
Trapping 20, *20*

Van Basten, Marco *27*, 77
Volleying 46-7, *46, 47*

Waddle, Chris 12, 27, 39, 77
Wales 24, 67
Wall pass 18-9, *18, 19*
Wallace, Gordon 18
Walls 68, *68*
Weir, Peter 76
West Germany *9*, 42
Whiteside, Norman 44, 68, *69*,
    76
Whyte, Chris 52
Wilkins, Ray 12
Winning the ball 54-5, *54, 55*
Wright, Mark 26